SIDETRACKED
IN THE WILDERNESS

SIDETRACKED
IN THE WILDERNESS

MICHAEL WELLS

Abiding Life Press

Published by Abiding Life Press
A division of Abiding Life Ministries International
P.O. Box 620998, Littleton, CO 80162

Fourteenth printing, March, 2012
Printed in the United States of America

Library of Congress Cataloging-in-Publication Data
Wells, Michael, 1952- 2011
Sidetracked in the Wilderness/Michael Wells.
p. cm.
ISBN 0-9670843-0-X
1.   Christian life—1960- 2. Wells, Michael, date. I. Title.
BV4501.2.W4182   1991
248.4—dc20   90-49987
                  CIP

Unless otherwise indicated Scripture quotations are from the New American
Standard Bible, Copyright the Lockman Foundation 1960, 1962, 1963, 1968,
1971, 1972, 1973, 1975, 1977.
Scripture marked NIV is from the HOLY BIBLE, NEW INTERNATIONAL
VERSION. NIV. Copyright 1973, 1978, 1984 by Internations Bible Society.
Used by permission of Zondervan Publishing House. All rights reserved.

Cover designed by Bob Fuller of Fuller Creative.

TO my Compassionate God

CONTENTS

CONTENTS

PREFACE

Why is it that the Christian experience is so often characterized by overpowering sin, defeat, loneliness, strained relationships, and depression? Why is it that so many Christians are discouraged and disillusioned? Take heart! For the very weakest can embrace God's simple solutions with confidence; success will not depend on talent, ability, or intellect, but rather on Him.

This book is written for those who have been falsely labeled "average Christians," but who in reality are the very heartbeat of the Kingdom. It is not written to offend but to bless, not to uproot but to plant. The book is intended to be read in its entirety; if it is not, I fear that too many questions will arise which, if left unanswered, would give much ammunition to the enemy. I trust that through our blessed Savior's allowing the writing of this simple work, all of the defeated will be stirred to hope and victory and, in turn, enabled to point others to faith. Therefore, I commit the work into God's hands to be used as He sees fit.

Note from Betty Wells:

With the fourteenth printing came a new edition; the message was unchanged but Bob Fuller gave the book a new cover and I lightly edited the older version. Michael Wells did not stay to appreciate this new edition he had long wanted; he departed from this earth to be with the Lord on October 11, 2011. The Spirit who drove the words in *Sidetracked in the Wilderness* will continue to bring Life to their meaning to those who will read and take them to heart.

CHAPTER 1
The Christian Experience

I remember when I first came to know Jesus Christ as my own personal Savior—what a wonderful day that was! It was truly an experience of walking out of darkness into light. Who can describe the mystery of Christ in us and the delight brought through fellowship with Him? I remember going to sleep and smiling so much that the next day I would awaken to find myself still smiling; I had so much joy that my face was even beginning to hurt from the continuous happiness! Scripture memory was a delight with no effort whatsoever, prayer was ceaseless, and the constant praise for the wonder of God's creation all around was the course of the day. Anxiety, pessimism, and dread were something long past, vaguely remembered. In a phrase, God loved me and I knew it, basked in it, and abided in it. Oh, the glory of being a child of God!

Then it happened. As I was walking across the campus one morning in the spring of my junior year of college, someone asked me a very simple question: "What do you believe the Lord is calling you to do, Mike?"

Up to that point, I had never pondered the question, but to my surprise an answer came out: "God is calling me to minister to defeated Christians." I knew in that moment this was exactly God's plan for my life. I did not spend much time questioning this except to wonder at the very thought of there being defeated Christians. I have often thought that if I had known what such a calling meant, I would have argued with the Lord and asked for a different job description. For then I did not know that in order to minister to defeated Christians, I must become defeated myself.

My fall to the life of defeat that I lived for the next nine years took a relatively short time. Soon prayer had become a struggle, Scripture had lost its attraction, unconquerable sins appeared on all sides, and the emotional awareness of God had disappeared!

I coped with my defeats and failures in a variety of ways. I read self-help and how-to books which all promised to give me one-time relief. Those how-to books eloquently described my condition but sent me away powerless to escape. The more I read, the more frustrated, angry, and depressed I became. They told me of the great example of Jesus, how He prayed, fasted, helped others, worshiped, was devout, fed the hungry, and loved; then they told me to imitate Him! Did they not realize that I *wanted* to be like Jesus and I *wanted* to please God, but I simply could not? Did they not realize that if I could imitate Jesus, He would not have had to come?

Still suffering under the delusion that knowledge is the answer and the veiled promise that when one moves he will leave all problems behind and start over again, I decided to attend Bible school and then graduate school, where the emphasis was really quite simple: Success rested on my ability, intellect, talents, and appearance. If all of these could be perfected to some measure, I would be a success, being acceptable to God and to His people. How I envied the student or professor who could preach from the original Greek text. If only I had the natural ability to speak, to be witty, to be clever, if I could just sing or play an instrument, then I would be living the abundant life!

Maybe I could memorize the entire Bible as some had, ask the audience to pick a Scripture verse, and then quote the one before it and the one after it—yes, then I would have arrived.

There was, of course, great emphasis on a variety of programs. Many renowned speakers came and shared their recipes for success; we all took notes vigorously, knowing that each must be presenting the much-needed procedure. I knew that I would not be able to adhere to the program in my own life, but at least I could condemn others for not completing it and pin the blame on them for its failure. After all, if they were truly committed Christians they would do better. Little did I know that I was looking for something seen, something of this world, something that did not require faith, some type of magic formula to deliver me from myself as well as others from the same state of defeat.

Why was it that Christianity was so difficult for me? Why is it that many of us strive for years to attain spirituality through a sequence of methodologies, programs, and techniques; and when blueprints for success fail, we give up and resign ourselves to a life of mediocrity, frustration, and regression? Is this the abundant life of which our Lord spoke? Did He speak of a life of turmoil, defeat, self-effort, endless entreaties for joy, and bondage to emotions, thoughts, and sinful behaviors for all who would dare to call upon His name? Was the life that He came to give to be characterized by conflict in families, endless trips to counselors, and depression so deep that many would wish to be taken out of this life in order to gain some measure of relief? I fear this is the prevalent Christian life for many, who often have heard the account of the Gospel in this way: Accept Jesus Christ today so you will not go to hell in the future. Yet after having accepted Him they hear, "Jesus died for your sins, now work hard to please Him."

The cry of many is, "I cannot please God; I cannot change. How do I get out of the hell in which I live daily?" For the majority of Christians, what has been made known through experience is only what does not work. One key word that would describe the Christian community around the world is *change*. We want to change what we are, what we do, and our circumstances so we will be acceptable to God, and yet after jumping through all the hoops prescribed by a particular method or program, change has not come, and we sense even more deeply our lack of acceptableness and failure.

If, then, it is so simple to live a defeated life, would it not be good news that it is equally easy to live the victorious life? What is the answer? It will be found in the simplicity of the Gospel, a simplicity that has been lost in the shuffle of programs, methods, and how-to lists, all symptoms of unbelief! The answer is not something that we must do but rather something we must believe. The great secret of success that has been concealed from the majority of Christians far too long is this: Christian growth is simply accepting what we have always had from the beginning, from the first day we gave our lives to Christ! This simple life—the victorious life—will be experienced only through the abiding life.

Abundant life is not something to work for, but rather is something given to be worked from. My acceptance is based not on what I do but rather on what I am. Abundant life does not require that I imitate Jesus, but rather that I participate in His life; it does not require that I work to believe, but that I work because I believe. Be assured of this: If the abundant Christian life requires great determination, self-will, intellect, talent, and ability, then we are all too weak, blind, and stupid ever to arrive.

How do I experience this life abundant? How do I discover a life free from sin? How can it be mine without effort? God's answer is specifically designed to be within the grasp of the weak, the failure, the unacceptable, the ignorant, the frustrated, and the hopeless. The answer is the simplicity of the abiding life.

God's answer for abundant life will always be unbelievably simple: The Christian must learn to believe and receive its simplicity. His answers require faith—faith we may not know we possess—not great talent, ability, or intellect. The problem is not that God places on us a great and difficult task to perform in order to experience His rest, peace, and joy. On the contrary, the problem is that we place on ourselves these great tasks and set for ourselves a standard of acceptance that is higher than God's. Therefore, all who would enter into the life of faith and rest must first experience the struggle and failure that come from their own effort to change. We will only give up on ourselves and turn to God's simple answer after we have exhausted every other conceivable resource. *God's answer is simple, but in order for Him to bring us to a place of accepting it, He must first put us through a series of courses that will exhaust us, leaving us despairing of self and others and prepared to listen to whatever God says with a believing heart. It is not until man refuses to trust himself that he will begin to trust God.* Many defeated Christians are merely in the process of learning to give up on themselves.

I began my Christian life in simple faith, standing at the foot of the cross. However, through unbelief I left that position, looking for capabilities within and trusting in self, much like Israel in the wilderness. The farther I journeyed from the cross, the more lost and confused I became until I decided to return to where I began; it was there that I found the simplicity lost! Have hope, for it is God's plan to bring all of us to a life of peace and joy. "If God is for us, who is against us?" (Romans 8:31)

Traveling around the world, I have found many godly believers who live a life desirable to all of us. One question that I immediately ask upon meeting such a one is, "How did you get to be such a spiritual person?"

The answer is always the same: "I do not know; God brought me this far." Not once has anyone told me it was because he belonged to a particular denomination or subscribed to a certain doctrine. It is rather because God brought him along, so take heart! God shows no partiality, and He will also take you where you need to go.

The following chapters do not contain any how-to lists, nor will they reveal methods one can follow to be assured of victory. In fact, they will give you nothing to do, since they are written to reveal what He has done and contain the steps that this child of God had to complete in his journey before he was willing to accept God's simple answer and begin to walk by faith. Through these steps God brought me to the end of trusting self and to the beginning of trusting Him, so I have regained the lost simplicity of faith and repossessed the joy that is mine in Christ.

So now, climb into the Father's arms; let Him carry you along the steps He has designed. All of your suffering is for a purpose, and though you do not see God's hand in it now, you will. When you see where He has taken you, you will break forth in praise. "As you do not know the path of the wind, or how the body is formed in a mother's womb, so you cannot understand the work of God, the Maker of all things" (Ecclesiastes 11:5 NIV). "But I am afraid, lest as the serpent deceived Eve by his craftiness, your minds should be led astray from the simplicity and purity of devotion to Christ" (II Corinthians 11:3).

"Father, we trust You to take us back to the simplicity of faith, the simplicity that made Abraham so pleasing to You, the simplicity that filled Your Son's life with joy, peace, and abundance unspeakable."

CHAPTER 2
Lost and Found and Lost Again

Jesus makes an appeal to follow Him on the assumption that what people are really looking for is rest. He knew that the crowds around Him were "weary and heavy-laden" (Matthew 11:28).

As we look around us we find many who appear to carry heavy loads. Each morning they have put on invisible backpacks filled with weights bearing different names such as *Husband, Wife, Children, Job, Finances*, and so on—making up the loads that they must bear. It is not necessarily bad to be tired, though, for as long as we are full of vigor we will not come to Him to receive our rest. Therefore, being tired is a good sign. If the father had found the Prodigal Son and replenished his funds one week before he ran out of money, how long would it have taken the son to return home?

What is it that causes mankind to experience such fatigue? We are not only tired from carrying that daily load of troubles, lost dreams, disappointments, and family problems, but we are also weary from looking for a savior to give us some relief from the heavy load. We have looked to our parents, friends, mates, and children, but since they are all looking to us for help, they never seem to get around to assisting. What we need is a supernatural Savior.

There will, of course, be no awareness for the need of a supernatural Savior who can meet our varied needs until the Holy Spirit has brought about the conviction of sin.

The juncture at which we acknowledge this conviction is usually preceded by an all-out attempt to save ourselves through a variety of methods, resolutions, and self-effort. By reaching this point, however, we have come to the inescapable conclusion that we cannot save ourselves and therefore are doomed. We have totally given up on ourselves to become better! In short, we have found ourselves in the world without hope.

The nation of Israel had come to a similar resignation before Christ began His ministry. During the time of sacrifices in Jerusalem, thousands of animals were sacrificed; it was said that a literal river of blood would flow from the temple. Each year the devout made the journey to Jerusalem, and each year, no matter how hard they had tried, there were always more sacrifices to be made. These people were always made aware of the judgment that rested on them because of sin. Is it any wonder that when John the Baptist appeared preaching a baptism of repentance for the forgiveness of sins that "all the country of Judea was going out to him, and all the people of Jerusalem; and they were being baptized by him in the Jordan River, confessing their sins" (Mark 1:5)? And yet, John's baptism was a baptism of despair. Imagine being controlled by a terrible sin, which if lifted would allow perfect service, and hearing that by being baptized by John we would be forgiven. Of course we would rush to the Jordan with the masses and be baptized! The joy, nevertheless, would be short-lived, because even though we were forgiven of sin, we were not given power over it, and so we would once again find ourselves slaves in need of forgiveness and without hope.

Once we have come under the conviction of the Holy Spirit and given up on our ability to save ourselves, we are ready and willing to allow Christ to become our Savior. We become, in a word, dependent. We acknowledge that we cannot live without Him. We are now His through a simple confession of faith. The Holy Spirit has done His perfect job of convincing us that we need a Savior. What a glorious discovery! What a relief to have pardon of sins!

Our feeling is that if Jesus could forgive us, then He can do anything at all. He will take care of us, and our families, and alleviate our discomforts and all those little vexing problems of life.

A new Christian is so full of faith, believing that God can do anything, that God does in fact do much for him. His new life can be likened to a honeymoon; all he cares about is pleasing his Savior. The terms *work* or *do* never enter his vocabulary, for all he is commanded takes place naturally out of love, with no effort involved.

God is the new believer's all, and because Jesus is coming soon, the young Christian must share this newly found joy with others; he must find the other lost sheep! Surely others would want to know what he knows. It does not take long before he meets the rejection of the world and finds that others are not so excited about the message, but so what? The world is a big place; there are so many who need to hear! What fun there is in witnessing, learning, prayer, and service; and the most beautiful thing is that it is all done without command.

Slowly, almost imperceptibly, the honeymoon ends. Ever so subtly the new believer takes his eyes off the Savior and sees only the "to do's." His prayers revolve more and more around himself. In fact, before he knows it, self becomes the most important thing.

As impossible as it seems, and no matter how weary he becomes, he strives for a perfection that somehow must be attained. Gradually he focuses less and less on Jesus and more and more on the "successful Christians" he has heard about, those who followed the right teachings or correct sequence of events and are living a life of joy, victory, answered prayer, and wonderful emotional experiences. But try as he might to regain his joy through sound teaching, suitable experiences, or just plain being right, it does not work. Even though he continues to strive, there is the overwhelming feeling that he lost something that may never be found again.

As Andrew Murray said, "If you must work to be something, you prove yourself not to be that thing at all." In this condition the believer may even feel that he is lost again. He knows Christ is the answer, and he wants to please Him, but he feels that he cannot. In many ways he is more miserable than he was before he was saved.

It reminds me of the wino at the mission when asked if he wanted to accept Christ. He opened a bottle of wine and answered, "No, thanks! I have enough trouble already."

In order not to give up, out of desperation the believer attends all the more conferences and seminars, reads his Bible, prays, fasts, and, of course, vows to do better, all in the hope that these gyrations will bring the promised relief! Somehow deep inside he realizes that he is like an automobile with a flat tire; every morning he puts air in the tire, but alas! By evening the air is out again, and he screams within, "Will someone please fix the hole?"

The journey from lost to found and back to feeling lost again can take a relatively short time. Remember Israel coming out of Egypt? The people left full of hope and faith in God. In the short distance to the Promised Land they stopped putting their hope and faith in God and instead trusted in themselves. They turned inward to what they thought they could accomplish. The end result was banishment to the wilderness, where they had to learn particular lessons that would once again turn their hope and faith to God.

Few Christians make the journey without wavering; for those we praise God. This book is not written for those believers but for those of us who have been sidetracked in the wilderness. The greatest lesson to be learned there is what does not work. Remember, we are making progress when we can find those things that do not work and exclude them.

CHAPTER 3
What Does Not Work

The first trip that I made around the world visiting a variety of countries and unique cultures was grueling and exhausting. Often I spoke three times a day. The time spent with and love received from my brothers and sisters in these faraway places supplied me with much more energy than was expended. How phenomenal it was to be treated as a part of the family, given the best seat, invited to share in the choice meal, and given the optimum sleeping quarters only because I bore the name of Christ. We truly are the family of God! On that particular trip I had the opportunity to speak to gatherings of dozens of differing denominations, many of which I had never heard before, and each with its own peculiar emphases. While discipling within the ranks of each denomination, I found the same amount of defeat and despair. I came to the conclusion that particular doctrine—held so dear by each denomination—was not producing the abundant life that it was supposed to; it did not work! It is relatively easy to be disfellowshipped from any denomination; all one need do is disagree with that group's chosen correct teaching. I believe in right and true teaching, but why is it that those who rest secure in their right teaching seem to be living on the same level of defeat as those who do not hold to such teaching?

Strong discipleship practices give a list of what to do for every conceivable situation. They function under the presupposition that people fail because they do not know what to do. But even in these very disciplined groups, those at the very top are not able to uphold all the rules and lists and ultimately fall by the wayside in defeat. The real issue is avoided. The lists of what to do to be spiritual and to change did not work!

To the same degree that man loses his God-consciousness, he increases the rules by which he lives. Volumes of ordinances indicate one thing: We do not know God personally. The Old Testament law was given for this very reason: Man did not know God. The Pharisees were an excellent example of this principle at work! The more God-consciousness they lost, the more their edicts increased.

I did some reading on Jewish dietary laws. In one article the author was emphatic that we Christians must not eat such meats as rabbit and camel. The question that immediately came to my mind was, "If I no longer eat rabbits and camels, will I get along with my wife better, will my children grow up knowing the Lord, and will I be able to overcome my depression and defeat?" The answer is obviously no. We should discuss something that will enable us to execute important acts influential toward our quality of life. When faced with wonderful theory, good-sounding teaching, laws prohibiting, or innovative frames of reference, I believe that we rarely ask ourselves the question, "Does this work?" We are so miserable in our present condition that we are willing to listen to anything that promises a quick remedy. At various times I have been told that Christians are not to own televisions, radios, open-toed shoes, wire-rimmed glasses, brightly colored clothing, or an organ in the church building. But in the ranks of the legalists have been found the grossest of immoralities. It must not work!

There has been much debate in the past over the issue of being filled with the Spirit and speaking in tongues. I have personally discipled teachers on both sides of the issue who are experiencing the same forms of bondage and sin. The point is that one can find among the defeated both those who speak in tongues and those who do not; either way must not ultimately be the solution to defeat.

The defeated can be found among those who were baptized in the "proper" manner at the "proper" time, who are submitting to spiritual authorities, who lead shepherding groups, who have whole books of the Bible memorized, who promote devotional and quiet times, who are tireless evangelists, who maintain levels of separation from the world, who make positive confessions, who read only the King James Version, who will not own a piano, and who have read all the good Christian books on parenting. We believe the words of Jesus, "You shall know the truth, and the truth shall make you free" (John 8:32). Obviously, those things we are mentioning are not *the* Truth, for those who practice them are not free.

The believer who is seeking a method to bring relief to his paltry state will rarely ask himself, "Where is Jesus in all of this?" In fact, if he would take the time to listen, he would notice that he was hearing less and less of the precious name of Jesus and more and more of what men exalt. When presented a particular scheme that promises to bring success, the Christian should always ask the question, "Could a committed Buddhist, Hindu, or Muslim accomplish this?" If the answer is yes, then there is nothing supernatural about the method; it is merely the teaching of man.

Some have been told that the source of their problem is demonic. Hours have been spent casting the demon(s) out, and yet within a few short weeks these people are experiencing the same condition of bondage to a particular sin or behavior as before. They are instructed to go through the exorcism once again, and then again, but with the passing of time they find themselves unchanged.

Much knowledge has no practical application to the hearers' lives. As I look at my Study Bible I notice that there is one full page devoted to the authorship of Isaiah. Was it one author or two? There is another page devoted to the authorship of Hebrews. Was it Paul or Barnabas? There is a guide to theology, and a special section on eschatology and the different views of the end times. Considerable time was spent on the research, and no doubt the most brilliant scholars were utilized, but why? Are these the things that concern the defeated who are in bondage? Do they carry significance for the oppressed Christian in China, the brother imprisoned in Nepal for baptizing a man, the Indian sister who does not have a meal this night, or even for you?

The Church is cluttered with shipwrecked scholars who thought the Bible was written for understanding and did not recognize it was written to give life. Some pastors urge their listeners to take notes during their sermons, but we do not need more filled pieces of paper; we need power. The Scriptures are searched to find knowledge, and the end results are broken marriages, rebellious children, and admitted lack of abundance.

God is not to be systematized and understood; that is something that unbelievers do to God. Rather, He is to be obeyed and worshipped. I have often thought that the wisest thing a theologian could do would be to sell his theological library, use the proceeds to buy a telescope, gaze up at the stars, and be silent. One evening spent this way will make anyone take his true position of ignorance before the Father of lights, experiencing what Job did. "Then Job answered the Lord and said, 'Behold, I am insignificant; what can I reply to Thee? I lay my hand on my mouth'" (Job 40:3, 4). There is a place for learning, but when it is a substitute for life it is a cursed thing. I have known some very brilliant men whose lives have become a mess. They and the ignorant, the talented and the ungifted, and the rich and the poor are all on equal footing when it comes to living the victorious life.

I am not saying that knowledge is not important. That is far from the truth; knowledge that leads to life is ultimately important, but again, if it takes the place of Christ and becomes the solution to daily life, it is a cursed thing. All knowledge needs to move eighteen inches lower than the brain into the heart!

I believe that many times the pursuit of knowledge keeps us from prayer. In fact, it is much easier to pursue knowledge than to pursue the Lord in prayer. We know that the Lord rules the world through the prayers of the saints, and yet in my personal travels I have not been to a single Bible college or seminary that offered a course in prayer. Where do we ultimately believe deliverance lies?

Because there are many hurting Christians in the Church, quite an interest has developed in Christian counseling. Many Christians hold vehemently that self-knowledge gained through psychological counseling is a concrete aid to helping the defeated enter into victory. However, one disturbing thing about some Christian counseling is that the Lord Jesus and His supernatural activity in our lives is often left out; the advice given to the Christian would suit the unbeliever just as well. True Christian counseling leaves a person looking to Christ, not to himself. I have always found puzzling the measure of hostility that can be raised among Christians when they hear Jesus is all we need. We are commanded to cast our anxiety on the Lord, not on psychology:

> ... I proclaimed a fast, so that we might humble ourselves before our God and ask him for a safe journey for us and our children, with all our possessions. I was ashamed to ask the king for soldiers and horsemen to protect us from enemies on the road, because we had told the king, "The gracious hand of our God is on everyone who looks to him, but his great anger is against all who forsake him." So we fasted and petitioned our God about this, and he answered our prayer.
>
> —Ezra 8:21-23 NIV

At some point are we also not ashamed for running to the world for the answers to the problems in man's soul?

Continuing our examination of what Christians try that does not work, we hardly need to mention all of the methods and programs that have been thrust upon us by those in the churches who have developed one campaign after another to increase the numerical size of the congregation. In many ways, the manner in which churches operate today is no different from the pyramid system many secular organizations employ. The emphasis is on getting more people in at the bottom and never being concerned with servicing those already in place. Often such practices are merely calculated to build empires for those who are the developers, who follow basic corporate formulas calculated to make them successful.

Many churches can be likened to hospitals that lack

competent doctors but are full of sick people, and the perceived solution to having so many ailing is to build larger hospitals that will accommodate more of the unhealthy, when what is really needed are a few more doctors to treat those already there.

How did our Christian life become so difficult? We were walking in the love of Christ but now find ourselves keeping a variety of "new moons" (Colossians 2:16). What has happened to the simplicity of which Jesus spoke when He likened believers to little children?

The root of all these methods may be quite easily determined. You see, we are commanded to live as depicted in chapters 5, 6, and 7 of Matthew. As we try, we find we simply cannot do it. Therefore, we develop a Christianity that we can observe, one in which we can exalt ourselves and judge others who cannot arrive at our level. If we find intellectual pursuits easy, we make proper doctrine, principled church order, and discipline all-important. On the other hand, if we find intellectual pursuits unattractive, then our Christianity might revolve around emotional experiences, and those whose experiences do not match ours are viewed as less spiritual.

In short, defeated believers are looking for the right thing—victory, a deeper life, something that will please God—but they are looking in all the wrong places.

One Indian brother tells the story of a man who lost the key to his house and, finding himself locked out, began to look for it under the streetlight. As the neighbors noticed the man they would ask what he was doing, and one by one they joined him in his search. Finally one of the neighbors asked the man, "Exactly where did you lose the key?"

The man replied, "Over there by the house."

The neighbor responded, "If you lost the key by your house, why are we all looking under this light?"

The man answered, "I could not see well enough where I lost it; I can only see under this light."

The believer who has lost his joy and victory in Christ too often looks where things appear to be clearest, not at the source of his defeat. Looking and looking in the wrong places never yields the key to success, and just because there is a measure of light, this is no reason to continue.

The Tree Ever Growing

What is the source of all these supposed solutions for our problems? The answer is found in the Garden. "And out of the ground the Lord God caused to grow every tree that is pleasing to the sight and good for food; the tree of life also in the midst of the garden, and the tree of the knowledge of good and evil" (Genesis 2:9). It is that last tree from which Adam and Eve ate, that forbidden tree from which mankind continues to eat. Let us look for a moment at the effects of that tree on all of humanity.

First we must understand God's criterion for accepting us, based on a pass/fail system. We pass and are accepted by Him if we are found to be in Christ; if, on the other hand, we are found outside of Christ, then we fail. This is all rather plain and simple until we decide to eat anew from the tree of good and evil; when this happens, God's simple truth is once again distorted and difficult.

Let us divide the tree in two, good on one side and evil on the other. If a man eats from the evil side of the tree and commits evil deeds, what does God do to him? The obvious answer is that He rejects this one whose deeds are unrighteous and who has fallen below God's standard of being in Christ. But if a man eats from the good side of the tree and does many good works, what will God do? Will He accept him and his good works? On the contrary, God will reject him, also, because his works have added to God's standard of being in Christ, and the man has committed acts of self-righteousness. God commands righteousness of us, and yet we are told every righteous deed is like a filthy garment. Good and evil come from the same tree and are treated alike by God—rejected. ". . . Darkness and light are alike to You" (Psalm 139:12). Doing evil is a sign of disbelief that God exists or will judge, but doing good is a sign of unbelief in God's standard of acceptance. We prove that we do not believe God at all when we add to this standard. We are touching upon one of the greatest deceptions in Christianity. God does want us to do good works, but what makes a work fitting is not the content but the origin; if the source of the work is faith as Christ expresses Himself through us, then it is acceptable. First Thessalonians 1:3 mentions work produced by faith, which is acceptable. But all other work is unacceptable, based on unbelief and self-righteousness.

Jesus recognized that the tax collectors and sinners, who had all eaten from the evil side of the tree, would often be given to repenting, because they could recognize that they had done wrong (they knew it, and so did everyone around them). However, Jesus did not hold the same hope for the Pharisees and teachers of the Law. The tax collectors and sinners would enter heaven before those who had eaten from the good side of the tree and could not see that they really needed to repent as much as the others. No one around them would testify to how truly repulsive and unacceptable their good works and self-righteousness were. There is a deep blindness that comes from eating from the good side of this forbidden tree.

In Matthew 23: 13-27, Jesus explains the results of adding to God's standard of acceptance. ". . . you shut off the kingdom of heaven from men; for you do not enter in yourselves, nor do you allow those who are entering to go in"; it brings lust after the things of the world: ". . . you devour widows' houses," and fraudulence, "even while for a pretense you make long prayers . . ." You ". . . make one proselyte; and when he becomes one, you make him twice as much a son of hell as yourselves"; i.e., men were doing bad/bad, but now have been persuaded to do the deceptive good/bad! It breeds "fools and blind men," who make lists and methods for men to follow which cause them to neglect "justice and mercy and faithfulness." All that matters is keeping the rules, while crucial matters are concealed. "You blind guides, who strain out a gnat and swallow a camel," ". . . you clean the outside of the cup and of the dish, but inside they are full of robbery and self-indulgence." Men may appear righteous because of their judgment toward others, but in reality they are "whitewashed tombs which on the outside appear beautiful, but inside they are full of dead men's bones and all uncleanness." As we can see, the deception from eating from the good side of this tree is in many ways worse than doing evil.

John 3:16 reads, "For God so loved the world, that He gave His only begotten Son, that whoever believes in Him should not perish but have eternal life." Our minds understand and accept the words. But listen to how the verse is read with the emotions of one who has been nibbling from that cursed tree. "For God so loved the world that He gave His only begotten Son, that whoever does not sin, lust, or have an evil thought, whoever reads his Bible, always attends church, never yells at the kids, prays, memorizes Scripture, does not own a radio, witnesses to the neighbors, gives, has spoken in tongues, has had a conversion experience, and is continually pure will not perish but have eternal life." Do you see the difference in eating from this tree? It obliges us to add an endless list for our acceptance by God, and in turn to put this big bundle on others' shoulders to carry, one which we ourselves cannot.

Eating from the tree will cause us to advocate a very simple teaching that goes like this: You did evil, now do good. We find the elements of this tree in Confucianism, Buddhism, Hinduism, Mormonism, Jehovah's Witnesses, and every other world religion. Witches study the evil side of the tree to gain more knowledge of evil; some so-called theologians study the good side of the tree to gain more knowledge of good, but there is no lasting difference between the two. Again, the question must be asked, are today's teachings yielding more additions to God's standard or promoting performance that would apply equally as well to the Hindu? Are they from the tree of the knowledge of good and evil, or are they from that other tree, the Tree of Life?

Suppose, because of God's leading, I decide to spend my Saturday helping my wife clean the house. It is the clear leading of the Lord that I do so. That may not appear to be very significant labor, and yet it will reap for me in heaven a rich reward! Why? Certainly not because of the magnitude of the work, but because of its derivation, which is His life in me. If we are living out of His life, we need not worry; the action, no matter how insignificant in our eyes, will always be good. On the other hand, I might preach to 10,000 for my own benefit, glory, and exaltation. This work will be hay, wood, and stubble burnt up on those last days! The magnitude of the work was tremendous, but the source was not Christ's life within but self-life.

Again, eating of the tree blinds us; many people do what the world considers to be great works that, to their surprise, will be burnt up in the end. I remember being confronted about this teaching by a very legalistic pastor who was quite adamant about his position of being righteous by his own works. His wife seemed very uncomfortable while he denounced false teachers and lazy Christians; she later revealed that they had left their last church because of an extramarital affair he was having.

The enemy loves to see us eat from this tree. Just as there are levels of evil for man to commit, so are there levels of good. Let us suppose that the evil a man can commit begins at one and progresses to ten on the negative side of the scale, as do the levels of good on the positive side. Let us imagine that when a man gave his life to Christ, he had been living at a minus-five on the evil scale. Now that he is a Christian, to what level of good do you suppose he will want to attain to be considered spiritual? I presume that he would strive to arrive at a plus-five on the good scale. The problem is that to the level of good one arrives, to that same level of evil he will tend to fall, so before he knows it he is back down to a minus-five. We see this principle among the Pharisees, who arrived at a plus-ten on the good scale by following all their rules, but how far did they fall on the minus scale? To a minus-ten, for they advocated crucifying the Son of God. This principle is at work among all legalistic teachers; the greater they place above God's standard, the farther they fall.

Some believers maintain that if they lived in a country where there was no physical persecution, they would be able to live a much more godly and productive life for Christ. Others believe that if they did not have so much religious freedom and had to be persecuted, they would be much more dynamic; in fact, they see persecution as a shortcut to maturity. God shows no partiality; the person who is persecuted must struggle with self-life just as the person who is not persecuted. There are no shortcuts to spirituality, but neither are there ever any physical hindrances to it. Spirituality comes from the Spirit of Christ, not from a certain set of circumstances. Constantine's tutor watched as the Church began to be accepted and commented that the world's love would replace its hatred as her enemy. Here we have one of the deep deceptions of the enemy, who would always have us looking to another place and time for what we want, as he hides from us that today, in this moment, there are no hindrances to spiritual growth and maturity. Why do we listen to him? It is that cursed tree!

Since so few are acquainted with God's pattern of acceptance and what that means for how they are to live their lives, it is easy for the enemy to toss us back and forth on the scale from plus to minus. God's ideal in terms of the scales we have just been discussing is a zero. Yes, we are successful Christians when we are living at zero!

But again there is difficulty, for I fear we have allowed others to define zero for us. We naturally assume that if we get up in the morning and our emotions are at a minus-six, then we must begin to plead with God until they arrive at a plus-six. We have allowed the enemy or others to tell us that our emotions should be at a plus-six, so we ask Him to appear to us in our living rooms; we confess, repent, wallow in guilt, and perform a multitude of other gyrations all in hopes of getting feelings to a plus-six. In so doing, we pass right through zero, where God wants them, and if we do drive them to a plus-six, it will not be long before they are once again at a minus-six. The world would describe this as bipolar manic depression, a big name for eating from the tree of the knowledge of good and evil.

The same thing happens with the mind. We decide not to think certain thoughts; no matter what, we will discipline our minds. So up the scale we go until, without warning, we find ourselves dwelling on the very lust, doubt, or dread at the same level of intensity with which we vowed not to think about it.

In the area of bodily desire we vow we will not eat, we will not eat, and then with corresponding frenzy we eat everything in sight!

What is living at a zero in our minds and emotions? What does it mean to have our emotions and thoughts following God's outline? We will have more to say of this later, but for now we can partly understand where our emotions are to be by discerning what is not supernatural. The supernatural life is manifested in the small, often unseen areas of our lives in such things as peace, mercy, and lack of condemnation when wronged. The first few miracles that Moses performed were duplicated by Pharaoh's magicians. In the same way, Satan can duplicate the large, spectacular signs and visions by which many judge spirituality. We must remember that we have a relationship with our

God, but many have made this relationship out to be one continual mountaintop experience after another, and the drive to continue to duplicate these experiences has exposed them to all kinds of deceptions, not to mention a general dissatisfaction with their own lives.

I have a relationship with my wife which I enjoy very much and which encompasses several different aspects. I enjoy the romantic involvement as well as simple activities done together: taking a walk at night, sitting in bed and reading, or taking a ride. There is also the quiet confidence that comes when she is upstairs working and I am below in the study, and there is the joy I have in hearing her voice on the phone when I am away. One of the greatest pleasures is knowing that even when I cannot see her, she is waiting for me. Most of my relationships with her are not physically or emotionally ecstatic, and yet they are all equally enjoyed.

I am not saying that God never stirs our emotions, but rather that most of us have never learned to rest in a relationship with the Lord when it is calm and quiet. We want more and more. If God is not inclined to stir our emotions or thoughts, then we will find artificial means to stimulate them. This is all the more compounded in the groups that only give glowing, spectacular reports about what the Lord is doing and what great things they are hearing. These people have come to believe that our relationship with the Lord is to be a continuous climactic arena, and they cannot rest and enjoy the simple aspects of their relationship with the Creator.

This becomes particularly confusing when it comes to knowing the will of God, which many strain for years trying to discern. The problem is that they are waiting for confirmation in their emotions, some vision, a dream, or a loud, distinct voice. Here is a great secret: When we are in the perfect will of God, we hear and feel nothing.

When my child is doing my will, he hears nothing from me. Suppose I have told him not to ride his bicycle in the street; if I see him doing it I will yell at him, and if he does not hear me I will run to retrieve him. However, if I look out the window and find him riding on the sidewalk as he is supposed to, he will hear nothing from me.

The same is true with the Lord. When we are in His will, we hear nothing. How does one get in His will? The process is really quite simple. When alternatives arise, one must say, "Lord, I want Your will, not mine. I have decided to move to such and such a place; if this is not Your will, please close the door. If it remains open, I will move ahead with confidence." A friend of mine wisely advises that after one makes a decision he should wait prayerfully seven days before acting, giving God a chance to close the door. You see, He is the Creator and we are the creatures; we make our God much too small if we cannot trust Him to direct our paths.

Many struggle over prayer, not knowing how to pray or hear God. They lie on the floor waiting for God to speak, or give up in frustration, having only one-sided communication with Him. Prayer is simple when experienced at zero and is more hearing than talking. The talking part comes as we let requests be made known to God; the hearing comes as we rest before Him very quietly, slowly reading Scripture and allowing the Holy Spirit to speak. God's voice will not be human, audible, loud, overwhelming, or a supernatural movement in the emotions; it will very simply be God's voice, easily recognized by all His sheep.

Just as living at zero is not a continuous emotional high, neither is it a constant low. Many believe they are only near to God when He is convicting them; every time they speak of the Lord they must share how God confirmed to them what failures they are. Looking at them, an outsider would not consider becoming a child of God.

Elijah was commanded to go listen for the Lord's voice and give heed to how the Lord spoke to him.

> . . . And a great and strong wind was rending the mountains and breaking in pieces the rocks before the Lord; but the Lord was not in the wind. And after the wind an earthquake, but the Lord was not in the earthquake. And after the earthquake a fire, but the Lord was not in the fire; and after the fire a sound of gentle blowing . . . a voice came to him.
>
> — I Kings 19:11-13

In chapter 2 we learned that the evil we did brought misery, discomfort, and defeat; but in this chapter we learned that all the maneuvers instigated in the attempt to do good have brought an equal amount of misery, discomfort, and defeat. Most importantly, neither route requires faith. If you can see these things, you are ready for the next chapter.

CHAPTER 4
Unbelieving Believers

Is there any defeat, failure, instance of depression, anxiety, frustration, or sin that does not have at its root unbelief? I have asked this question to audiences all over the world and have yet to find one.

Once when I was in a small town in India, a woman asked if she could have some time alone with me in order that we might discuss her problems and look to the Lord for the solution. She had written on a small piece of paper the many items about which she was concerned, including questions pertaining to her unbelieving husband, her children, relatives, and, of course, her own personal struggles with the Lord. Her English was very poor and my Hindi was nonexistent, so I enlisted the aid of the pastor to translate for us. With every question, we opened the Scriptures and looked to the answer that God would give, each of which was Christ-centered and pointed her to a moment-by-moment relationship with the Lord, which I was persuaded would cure the problems. However, with each answer she would immediately ask another question. After over an hour of this routine, I realized that although this particular woman was reading her Bible and praying more than four hours each day, she was an unbelieving believer!

Let me explain that an unbelieving believer is someone who is a Christian, is born again, and will arrive in heaven; the problem is that this person has never believed in the Lord Jesus with his whole being. That is, with his mind he receives and believes all that is told him about the grace, care, concern, and love of the Lord Jesus; he is a believer. Yet at the same time, he feels that he is in charge of every aspect of his Christian life, that he must change the lives of those around him, bring transformations into his own life, and work to make himself pleasing to God. That is, in his emotions he is unbelieving.

The Church today is full of such unbelieving believers, who with their minds run to God but with their emotions run away from Him. Much time and effort have been spent persuading people's thoughts to agree with what Scripture says, but very little attention is given to the emotions, which need equal convincing; an emotional concept of God is just as important as the intellectual view. A negative emotional perception of God will hinder attempts to look to Christ as the Way, the Truth, and the Life. Many understand (believing) that God will care for their every need but feel (unbelieving) that He really will not help and they must do everything themselves, so they continue in great turmoil.

It must be very frustrating to the pastor who is preaching weekly to a congregation filled with unbelieving believers, for no matter how well the sermon is organized or what amount of power it exudes, it will accomplish nothing in the life of the listeners. Equally discouraged is the congregation that has an unbelieving believer as a pastor, for every sermon that is delivered will attempt to stir the assembly to action through guilt, manipulation, or intellectual argument. The lesson will always point to what the members must do to improve their condition, without emphasizing what Christ has already done to improve the malady.

It has been said that unbelief is the mother of every sin! When we feel the weight of concerns upon our shoulders, when we are once again courting the sin we thought long gone, when we are withdrawing from those who love us, and when we find ourselves returning to the world, is not unbelief the cause? Is it not the root of every evil? ". . . When the Son of Man comes, will He find faith on the earth?" (Luke 18:8)

The term *faith* is used over 230 times in the New Testament and is the central theme for those who would live the simple life of victory. Before we look at the source of unbelief, we must understand the effects of being unbelieving believers. Only then will we truly understand the "self" that is to be denied daily and the life of faith that will bring to naught the power of the unholy trinity: sin, Satan, and the world.

The Defeat of Unbelief

Let me now ask a very personal question: Are you saved? As we turn to the Scriptures we find that there are three things Christ has accomplished for us. First, through faith in Him we can be born again. Second, through His blood we can be forgiven, and third, through His life we can be saved. There is a difference between the three; a person can possess full inclusion in the first two without participating in the third! In fact, I believe that heaven will be filled with people who were forgiven and born again but never entered salvation in their daily lives. They are those who did not find Jesus as daily Savior from vexing sins that control, the guilt that follows, and the unavoidable, inescapable bondage.

To understand what the term *saved* means, we must

turn to the Old Testament. In most cases it refers to being delivered from present conflict, circumstances, and enemies. The people look for the God of their salvation. When they cry out, they need help *right then*, not at a subsequent time such as when they reach heaven. Being born again will get us into heaven (John 3), but we need salvation from the things that currently oppress us.

Listen to Paul's words in I Corinthians 1:18, "For the word of the cross is to those who are perishing foolishness, but to us who are being saved it is the power of God." He makes it clear that those who reject the message of the cross experience perishing today; he speaks in the present. The same, however, is true of the believer who embraces the message of the cross; that is, he will experience the saving power of the cross today ("who are being saved"). Being saved occurs in the present! How can that be? We are already assured of going to heaven, being forgiven and born again. Quite simply, the cross delivers us today from our current agony and all of the enemies pitted against us.

Paul again makes this clear in his letter to the Philippians (1:28; 2:12, NIV): "Without being frightened in any way by those who oppose you. This is a sign to them that they will be destroyed, but that you will be saved—and that by God"; and, ". . . continue to work out your salvation with fear and trembling." We see that salvation is something for the here and now.

Envision a man released from prison because the death sentence that he deserved is commuted by the act of another, such as the leader of the country. The man who is released and forgiven has a heart full of joy and thankfulness; he is, to say the least, relieved. But what of all the circumstances, events, bondage, sin—indeed, the very nature of the man—that brought him to such a place of being worthy of death? If these do not change, though the man is forgiven, his joy will not continue for long, and his repeating failure will cause his own heart to condemn him. This man not only needs forgiveness but freedom from all that took him to the point of death.

What would be the loss to my life if I believed that salvation is only for a future time? Very great, for I would continue to suffer defeat today, looking forward to freedom in the future, when all the while I could have lived in victory had I seen the Savior as Someone who delivers today and every day until the final deliverance from this body.

When we understand what *salvation* means, the words of the angel in Matthew 1:21 have all the more meaning to us: "And she will bear a Son; and you shall call His name Jesus, for it is He who will save His people from their sins." Salvation is to be a daily experience that must be supernatural. We must believe what the Savior exhorts in John 15:5, ". . . apart from Me you can do nothing." But if we are full of unbelief, then those words will in our minds sound like a blessing but in our emotions sound like a curse. Also, we will search for a savior other than Christ to free us from the bondage we are in. In this condition, we cannot help but look in all the wrong places!

The Idolatry of Unbelief

If there were one thing you could receive from the reading of this book, what would you want it to be? What is it that you need? I imagine that your answer would have some of the following integrated into it: love and the desire to have that deep loneliness you often feel satisfied with the joy of being loved and accepted, and you would also like some measure of security and assurance. All of our deepest needs are spiritual needs which God, and God alone, can meet. If, however, you are an unbelieving believer, then you have not been able to look to God to meet your deepest needs.

Where have you looked to have these needs met? How are you coping with the world around you? What do you do in the midst of the severest defeat? To whom or what are you turning when under extreme pressure? Where do you find comfort? How do you exist in a world where God is relevant only for the future (to keep you out of hell)? How do you live among a humanity that seems to be pitted against your every move?

Let us now examine the development of some coping mechanisms.

The Development of Idols

A coping mechanism is quite simply the world's term for an idol. An idol is anything other than Christ to which we run when under pressure. Whenever we are hurt, we must find some way of coping with that hurt. The thing that we run to when injured is our idol.

I once began discipling a very committed Christian who worked hard for the Church and was an active evangelist. His wife had decided that she would surprise him one evening when he was working; she packed up several treats and went to his private office. Upon arrival she found him on the phone making an obscene phone call; pornography was scattered everywhere.

The husband was brought to me because of his severe problem. The first thing I set out to do was to take a history of the man prior to his conversion. I found that when he was twelve, his father had become an alcoholic, and Saturdays were the worst day of the week for this boy. On that day his father would stay at home and begin drinking early in the morning; by noon he would be drunk and often fight with the boy's mother. On one occasion the boy witnessed his father's taking his mother by the back of her hair and pushing her face through a wall.

Can you imagine yourself in this position, watching your father and mother clash and not having the Lord Jesus to run to with this pain? What would you do to cope in such a situation? The boy ran and hid under his father's bed, and guess what he found? His father's pornographic magazines! Instead of spending afternoons with battling parents, he was able to spend time with naked women on the pages of a magazine, women who never rejected him. He found that as long as he was looking at those pictures, he no longer heard the discord. Soon pornography became this boy's idol; after all, it was one thing to which he could run when under pressure to get his mind off the problems in his family, and at the same time it offered pleasure, acceptance, and a sedative for the pain he was experiencing.

At age sixteen the boy became a Christian and put away pornography; he attended Bible college and seminary, and for many years he had nothing more to do with it. However, several years later he was under severe pressure; his children were rebelling, things were not going well at work, and he perceived problems in his marriage. If you were the enemy (Satan) and your job description was to kill, steal, and destroy, when you noticed that this man was under extreme strain, in what way would you tempt him? Of course, pornography! The enemy is not ignorant of our personal history, and he uses it to develop a temptation that is perfectly suited to us, luring with something that he knows will attract us. This man was enticed with pornography because in the past it had worked to relieve his hurts; thus, he would be susceptible to returning to it.

However, there is one major problem with renewing a love affair with idols of our past. God will not allow any idol to meet a Christian's needs! Yet we often refuse to give up on an idol simply because it worked so well in the past; this allows the enemy to stand behind us and tell us the reason the idol is not meeting our need as it did before is that we are not doing or using enough of it. For instance, he says, "The reason pornography is not working is that what I am looking at is not hard enough." So that man purchases more extreme pornography, and yet God does not allow it to meet the need. At this point, because of increasing pressure and the inability to find a sedative, the person becomes frantic. Christians who are using idols with which to cope are easy to recognize, for they manifest such symptoms as apprehension, uncertainty, dismay, distress, and depression. None of these will accompany the man of faith.

Beginning in Genesis 29, we read the story of Jacob and his quest to obtain Rachel as his wife from the unethical Laban. Jacob worked for Laban for seven years to marry Rachel, and yet at the end of the seven years Jacob was tricked and given Rachel's sister, Leah, instead. He then agreed to work for another seven years that he might acquire his beloved Rachel. At the end of this period, Jacob was persuaded to spend another six years in service to his father-in-law; during this time God prospered Jacob and gave to him riches that once belonged to Laban. At the end of Jacob's twenty-year tenure, he decided to take his wives, children, and flocks and depart. Rachel and Leah had been with Jacob for twenty years; they had watched as God had blessed them by giving them to Jacob; they had noticed that every evil thing that was done to their husband God had turned to good. They had experienced Jehovah's blessing on their families, and it was the custom that they serve the God of their husband. Why, then, when they were called out completely from the bondage of their father's house did they steal the household idols (Genesis 31:19)? Why did they hide the idols and take them along on the journey to which God had called them? It was because of unbelief! "Just in case God does not help us on this journey, we will have with us the idols of the past, which will surely assist us in time of need," must have been their reasoning.

The same is true of Christians today! God has called us to journey into the Promised Land, but we have hidden the idols of the past so that just in case God does not help us (according to our timetables and own ways), we have them to trust. The majority of Christians begin the journey into the life of peace, rest, and victory with a suitcase full of the idols of the past, those things that we trusted before we came to know Christ. "Those who cling to worthless idols forfeit the grace that could be theirs" (Jonah 2:8 NIV).

It has been said that there are only four types of people in the world. The first says, "I, not Christ!" This group includes such people as Buddhists, Hindus, agnostics, and atheists. The second says, "I and Christ!" These will let Christ be fire insurance to keep them out of hell but will take care of everything else themselves. The third type says, "Christ and I!" These are the most miserable Christians, for they want Christ to be Lord, and yet if He does not act according to their plan when they think He should, out come the idols. The fourth kind says, "Christ, not I!" Having learned the secret of dependence upon and trust in Christ alone, they enter into God's rest and cast all anxiety upon Him.

The Variety of Idols

Let us examine some of the more common idols, remembering that an idol can be anything, for it is what we run to other than Christ when under pressure or pain. As we were growing up, it was unavoidable that we experience a certain measure of unpleasantness, and, as stated before, for every hurt experienced an idol must be found to help cope with the pain.

Consider the adolescent girl who is growing up in a dysfunctional home in which divorce has taken place; she has been moved from one school to another, and her mother currently lives with a man who sees the teen as an unnecessary accessory. There are normally two elements composing any hurt; the first is pain and the second is rejection. We can safely assume that this girl will begin a search for something that will alleviate both. Working hard at the church will get rid of the rejection, in that many will praise her selfless efforts, but it will not cure the pain that she is feeling. Getting good grades and having her name appear on the honor roll at school will bring many positive strokes and rid her of rejection, but the pain will remain. Getting drunk or taking drugs will temporarily free her from pain but will probably fuel still more rejection, thus intensifying the hurt.

In fact, there is only one thing readily available to purge both pain and rejection, quite popular because it normally costs nothing monetarily, and we are assured covertly from all sides that it will indeed heal us of our hurt. That one thing is sex. While involved in the sexual act we receive pleasure and thus are free from our pain, while at the same time someone is holding us—even if just for the moment—and ridding us of that dreaded rejection. By the next day we may have pain *and* rejection intensified by this involvement, but advertising, movies, television, and friends all assure us that sex will sooner or later meet our need.

There are easily recognizable idols that are very ugly and repulsive; these come from the evil side of the tree of the knowledge of good and evil. There are, however, idols that do not appear to be all that bad at first glance. These are in many ways wilier because they are easily excused or accepted, or they are harmless or even beneficial when not used as substitutes for God. Included in this list are food, shopping, television, radio, clothes, control, lying, manipulation, withdrawing, contention, exploding, reading, slander, fantasy, and greed. A particular thing may be an idol for one person but not the next, depending on whether or not it is used to meet inner needs.

There are also "Grade A" idols, some even sought after by many in the Church as respectable; these are most dangerous of all. There can be an idol of ministry. That is, the wife tells a man that he is failing at home as a father and husband, so he withdraws to the Church where people will tell him what a wonderful job he does. There is the idol of theology, which seeks to justify its basis in unbelief by stripping God of all His miracles, personal work in the life of the believer, His known presence, and anything else that hints of being supernatural. Many invoke the idol of position, vocation, or travel. Not content to be mere Christians, they must have something that sets them apart from the masses. There is the idol of religion, whereby we let those around us know immediately that we have a hotline to God and are not common people as are they.

As you can see, we traffic in a variety of idols, some ugly, some acceptable, and some appearing to be very beautiful. We have only mentioned a few; many more are easily discerned by observing what the unbelieving believer runs to when under pressure.

The Failure of Our Idols

God will not allow His children to worship idols and, therefore, withholds His peace from those who do.

Israel came out of the bondage of Egypt by fixing her attention on the one true God. Why is it that the trip to the Promised Land took Israel so long to complete? Ezekiel gives us the clue: "But they rebelled against Me and were not willing to listen to Me; they did not cast away the detestable things of their eyes, nor did they forsake the idols of Egypt" (20:8). They refused to do away with the idols they had trusted during their captivity. We, too, had idols trusted during our captivity; however, when God through the grace of the Lord Jesus brought us out of darkness into His light, He wanted us to leave the idols behind.

Ezekiel was given a vision that told him to dig through a wall in the temple and describe what he saw. "So I entered and looked, and behold, every form of creeping things and beasts and detestable things, with all the idols of the house of Israel, were carved on the wall all around" (8:10). In the very temple of God, Israel had hidden her idols!

I often disciple believers who are struggling with homosexuality. On one particular occasion a man came to me and said, "You are my last hope!" I have learned that whenever anyone says that, he rarely has any intentions of getting well, for he puts the pressure of his getting better on my performance and not his own. As we began to share, I pointed out to him that homosexuality was nothing more than an idol, the driving force of which is rarely sex but acceptance. Even in a heterosexual relationship, contrary to what is popularly taught, sex for the man is much more emotional than physical. When he is rejected, it is a blow to his identity, not his sex drive. He feels unacceptable and worthless, then angry, depressed, and withdrawn. Hence Paul's command, "Stop depriving one another . . ." in I Corinthians 7:5. This particular man had been abandoned by a father he never knew. He hungered for male acceptance, which at age sixteen he sought and found, and with very little effort it turned into sex. Then acceptance and sex were intermingled and confused, the end result being that he was battling homosexuality.

I asked, "If you could take a pill that would not only deliver you completely from it but would also actually wipe homosexuality off the face of the earth, therefore making it an impossibility for you, would you take the pill?" He claimed that he would take it in a heartbeat. I then asked, "What do you do when things do not go well at work?" He said he went to the gay bar. "What do you do when you are bored?" He went off to the gay park! "What do you do when you have a fight with your wife?"

"I lie in bed and fantasize."

I then inquired, "If you take this pill that abolishes homosexuality, what will you do when things do not go well at work, when you are bored, or when you have a fight with your wife?"

His response was, "I really would not want to take the pill."

You see, many of us are miserable with our idols but not so much so that we do away with them. We have found some comfort in them and have no intentions of getting rid of them. In essence we are crying out, "Please take these from me, if you can pry them out of my cold, dead hand!"

How is it that we can turn from the living God, who gave His only Son to purchase us, to the things of the past that bound us without mercy? "What fault did your fathers find in me, that they strayed so far from me? They followed worthless idols and became worthless themselves" (Jeremiah 2:5 NIV). Why do we hold on to the very things that can never give us life? "My people have committed two sins: They have forsaken me, the spring of living water, and have dug their own cisterns, broken cisterns that cannot hold water" (Jeremiah 2:13 NIV). Many have found something they believe will help them and refuse to let go of it, even though it is merely a broken cistern that can never hold true life and must in the end fail them. We are so fond of the idols we have developed and trusted for so long that left alone we would never give them up. We would continue to place confidence in them during times of crises, not looking to our precious Father in heaven but continuing to play the prostitute. Therefore, God must do for us what He did for Israel, allowing us to wander in the wilderness and depend upon these self-made idols, which fail us over and over again until we cast them aside and once again make Him the focus of our lives.

The wilderness experience is not a joyful adventure for any of God's children; this defeat cycle is depicted in the Book of Judges. When the people of Israel were comfortable, they forgot their Creator; next they began to worship the idols that surrounded them, becoming miserable in bondage. At last they remembered who their true God was and cried out for deliverance, only to have the cycle begin all over again. Just as then, He must put His people in one miserable situation after another until we are forced to the conclusion that God alone must receive our full trust.

Once I was asked, "If I commit adultery will God still love me?"

My answer was, "Of course He will! In fact, He will love you so much that He will probably discipline you harshly for it."

The man looked at me with a rather strange expression, so I asked, "Have you ever noticed what a mother does to her child after she has snatched it from the path of an oncoming car?" Because of fear for the child and hope that the small one will never again go into the street without looking, the mother often chastises him or her.

When God notices that one of His children is utilizing the idols of the past, the loving Father will discipline out of the hope that His child might be redeemed and turn away from the cursed thing. God does not create calamity but is fully capable of using that which we create to His advantage in revealing the inadequacy of our idols, directing us to Himself, and thus deepening our faith.

Suppose someone has learned to cope with lack of natural ability by manipulating others to give him what he wants.

God might place him in a position where advancement is possible and needed, but He will not allow the idol of manipulation to work for him. This person will be driven to God for the meeting of his need.

Or imagine the woman who learned at a very early age that the more attractive she is, the more control she has over others. God may place her in a situation where she must compete on a basis other than outward appearance.

Or assume there is the man who always trusts intellect and reason and is constantly calculating the outcome of others' actions. God could withhold grace from such a man to the point that he does something so foolish that he will know that his natural intellectual reasoning of itself has no value.

It is quite easy to recognize those who are in this process, for their lives are characterized by constant frustration as a result of their faithful old idols' failing them. They cannot understand how these could have worked well for so many years and now all of a sudden are so disappointing.

Imagine that on a given occasion there is something I wish to do but am opposed. In the past when I wanted my way I was able to intimidate others into going along with me, so I immediately pull out the idol called "Intimidation," only this time no one seems to care; they hold their ground and I do not get my way. What will I do? I will probably try "Intimidation" one more time; after all, it worked so well in the past! If there is another failed attempt, then I will toss aside that idol and reach for another—perhaps "Stalking"—to give it a go. It is a very frustrating experience when the faithful idols of the past begin to fail, and frustration can often be followed by panic. This process can be even more frustrating if some counselor is trying to replace the failing idols with others which he believes will work better for me. All I do at that point is switch idols and prolong my misery.

What idols do you run to when under stress and pressure? What are these precious, hidden aids you have kept in a safe place to be used on that day when all else fails? Many have kept these secret for years, even preaching against and condemning those who practice the very same things. What are these "creeping things and beasts and detestable things"? We all have them, and, as believers, we are in the process of laying them aside.

One woman's husband had confessed that he was making plans to leave her. She tried everything to keep him: forgiveness, working harder, making herself more attractive, reading books, counseling, confrontation, anger, hostility, retribution, threats, and the excuse of the children. There was one thing, however, that she did not try—Jesus! It was not until she cast aside all of the idols she had trusted for years to keep her husband that the Lord alone brought him back to her. Later she told me she was grateful for the situation, because it revealed to her all the things she was trusting in other than God.

Are you tired of trusting false gods? Are you willing to give up all but the Lord Jesus Christ? If you are, then you are ready to enter into the Promised Land, the place of real rest, that domain where God is all in all. There you can find an end to the frustration, anxiety, distrust, dismay, and depression that so often accompany unbelief! If you are ready to cast aside the idols of the past, the way to do that is incredibly simple.

Casting Aside Our Idols

Unfortunately, many today have more faith in Satan's ability to deceive than in God's ability to hear and act, more confidence in Satan's proficiency in taking a believer away from God than in Christ's capability to keep. But this is not the case; our Father in heaven is infinitely more powerful than our enemy. All we need to tap into the power of the Father is simple faith, which begins with the words in our mouths.

The problem many of us have with faith is that if our experience does not immediately follow our request, then we believe God has not really heard us, and once again we offer up the prayer. Let me emphasize that the power in prayer is not in how it is said or in the person who utters it; the power of prayer rests wholly in the One who hears it, and it is the Father in heaven who has commanded us to beseech Him for one reason, that He might hear and answer.

We have made petitioning God much too difficult. Many lie prostrate on the ground, try to envision themselves in heaven, make appeals to see the Savior in order to be assured that He hears them, and the list goes on, leaving the casual observer to assume that these people do not believe that God is listening or answering at all. Prayer is simple; it is telling God what we want and presenting ourselves to God as no better or worse than we really are. The power in prayer is that God Himself hears us! That we may not feel He hears us means nothing.

If we were in my office, it would be a simple thing for me to give you my pen; I would simply hand it to you and it would be yours the moment you take it. Later on in the day I may find myself looking in my pocket for the pen because I feel that I still have it, but the fact is you accepted and have taken it. It is just that simple to give your idols over to God; you just hand them to Him.

Many, I fear, believe that giving something to God is analogous to throwing a pen in the air and then waiting for a moment while gravity brings it back down. When the pen is in the air they may feel God has it, so their responsibility is to keep it in the air, but it keeps returning to their hand. This is like a boomerang prayer; though offered to God, it keeps returning. The responsibility of seeing the prayer through to its answer keeps returning to them. It is not long before they become weary and give up altogether!

Let us imagine that you sign a contract with me agreeing to my ownership of all your earthly possessions. Just because I do not come for them tonight does not mean that I will not come at all. I simply may be in no hurry to claim them. They may remain in your house, but they have now become my property. The same is true of the idols that you give God. They may remain in your being, but remember that God has accepted them and will take them away as He sees fit.

I remember when I first gave God the idol of slander, and the next day I found myself slandering. I gave Him once again this idol only to find myself continuing to backbite. The next time I came before the Lord and turned over once more the idol of slander, He spoke to me and said, "I took it the first time." From then on when I stumbled, I would always thank God that He had heard me and taken the idol the first time.

Hannah Whitall Smith suggested that we take our

burdens and cares, write them on a piece of paper, and give them to the Lord once and for all. I have often advised others to do this, then hold the list up to the Lord with both hands. It will not take long before that small piece of paper has taken on greater weight. In fact, as one holds his arms high to the Lord, allowing Him to see all that is written, the arms will soon feel as though they are trying to lift the weight of the world. Next, if this person thinks of that idol that has been trusted to meet needs, will it help now? Will drunkenness, drugs, food, controlling, withdrawal, status, or material gain make that little piece of paper any lighter? One should realize that he simply was not created with the ability to carry all his concerns, and nothing he has trusted so far has come to his aid.

Remember the Jews who wanted Jesus to depart from their territory once He had allowed the demons to enter into their pigs so that they rushed headlong over a cliff? Why were those people so upset with Jesus? They were not supposed to own pigs anyway! Do any of us really have the right to possess even one of the idols that have been mentioned? Can those who fight so hard to gain the privilege to be homosexual, have abortions, produce pornography, gain large settlements, divorce, and so on really say in all honesty that these rights have brought joy and serenity?

A brother in Christ who once came to me for discipling had a very severe physical condition which made him quite uncomfortable. During the course of our conversation, I asked if he had given to God his desire to get well. He did not immediately understand, and I explained that he must be willing to be in that physical condition the rest of his life. His worship and love of God could not carry any price tag, but the evidence that it did was his indignation over not having been delivered. The brother became angry and left, stating that God should heal him! A few days later he returned glowing, reporting that the previous night he had lain before the Lord, given Him his right to get well, and immediately was made well.

Hindered by Your Concept of God

One of the greatest weaknesses in Christianity today is that we ask a person to accept Jesus Christ into his life or we tell the defeated Christian to make Him Lord without taking the time to find out whom the unbeliever *feels* he is making Lord. We thank God for evangelistic campaigns and the fruit that God has borne through them; however, we must ask why it is that out of the thousands who come forward to accept Christ into their lives, only a small percentage continue on in the Lord. It is because during the one hour of the meeting, mind (intellectual belief) overruns emotions (emotional unbelief), allowing a person to go forward and make a public profession. However, within a few weeks emotions once again overcome the mind, and the convert becomes complacent and begins to turn away from the Lord.

I would like you to take a simple test whereby we might, through the leading of the Holy Spirit, discern your emotional concept of God. The test is not to be answered on the basis of what you know but by how you *feel* at your worst moments. It is a depressing thought, but what you are at your worst moment is your true condition. A wife does not know what she is like when her husband brings her flowers, but only when he knocks a quart of milk off the table with his elbow. A husband does not know what he is like when his wife has done all that he desires, but rather when she is thirty minutes late picking him up from work.

I once asked a brother who had been a missionary for twenty years this question, "When you think about being with God, what do you feel?"

He answered, "Love!"

I responded that this was the same thing that I had learned in Bible college, but I was not asking what he *knew*, but rather how he *felt* at his worst moments, when he was lying in bed and the whole world was caving in. He started cursing God! You see, there was a great difference between what he knew intellectually and what he felt emotionally.

The following test is designed to discern how you feel about God at your worst moments, so please, when answering the following questions do not make them more difficult than they are; simply write down the first answer that occurs to you.

1. When I think about being with God, I feel . . .
2. When I have to trust God, I feel . . .
3. When I think about God, I wish . . .
4. Sometimes I get angry with God when . . .
5. It frustrates me when God wants me to . . .
6. I really enjoy God when . . .
7. The one thing I would change about myself to please God is . . .
8. When I think about God's commands, I feel . . .
9. Sometimes I wish God would . . .
10. I can really depend on God when . . .
11. In my relationship with God, I am always sure that He will . . .

12. The one thing that frightens me most about God is . . .

13. God surprises me when . . .

14. One thing I am afraid God will do is . . .

I have given this test in several countries with varying cultures, and the answers from defeated and struggling Christians appear to be fairly consistent. The typical answers are as follows:

1. When I think about being with God, I feel *fear, loneliness, that He is not there.*

2. When I have to trust God, I feel *like He really will not help me.*

3. When I think about God, I wish *I could see Him or that He would change me.*

4. Sometimes I get angry with God when *He does not seem to hear me, He leaves me alone, He does not help.*

5. It frustrates me when God wants me to *do the impossible, which He always does. He gives me commandments I cannot keep.*

6. I really enjoy God when *He forgives.* (If people really enjoy God when He forgives and they are not experiencing much joy, we can safely conclude that they really do not believe that He does forgive!)

7. The one thing I would change about myself to please God is *everything.* (This answer reveals feelings of being unacceptable to God, of needing to do more for God.)

8. When I think about God's commands, I feel

inadequate, because I so often have not been able to keep them, or judgment for failing.

9. Sometimes I wish God would *take me home.* (This person is saying, quite simply, that life with the Lord has been miserable!)

10. I can really depend on God for *nothing.*

11. In my relationship with God, I am always sure that He will *judge me, get me, reveal to everyone my faults.*

12. The one thing that frightens me most about God is *His judgment.*

13. God surprises me when *He answers or is there.*

14. One thing I am afraid God will do is *kill someone I love to get my attention.*

God, and God alone, can meet our deepest needs; we all recognize this in our minds, but what about in our emotions? Is there anything in our emotions that might keep us from running to God to have these needs met, thus embarking us on an endless journey trying to find that one person, that special thing, that incredible place, yes, that adored idol that will meet our needs? Look at how God is described by the defeated Christian in the test above. Although we know that God is none of the above, the defeated Christian often *feels* that this is who is being prayed to, worshiped, and trusted to meet needs.

Imagine attending one of the large evangelical meetings and, after hearing a tremendous message on the saving life of Christ, being asked to come down to the front to accept Him as your personal Savior. Then picture the key speaker following up his invitation by describing the emotional concept of Christ that we have gleaned from the test above! He would explain that by accepting Jesus into your life, from this day forward you will have fear and no help, God will not be there, He will not hear you, it will be impossible to keep His commands, God will judge you, you will be unacceptable, and He may even kill someone in your family to get your attention! Would you or those around you go forward after such an invitation? We do not take seriously that many reject the Lord not on the basis of what is heard but what is being felt.

I once met with a very intellectual agnostic who despised Christians; after I mentioned that I was one, he immediately informed me that Christians were ignorant, unlearned, superstitious, and most insincere in their quests for holiness. Since we were traveling together and had some time, I asked if he would do me the honor of taking my test. He did, and his answers were similar to those we have seen in the test above; his emotional conviction was that God was not there, would not help, would bring harm, and would never listen to him. After showing him his emotional concept of God, I said, "If that really did describe God, then I would want nothing to do with Him either. In fact, I would start making up excuses to stay away from Him!"

He then answered, "Well, all Christians are hypocrites." I told him that was one excuse. "Well, they are all money hungry, too." That made two reasons. "All they care about are buildings." Three. "They never help anybody." That was the fourth excuse to stay away from God. He gave several more rationalizations, but I could certainly understand his need to do so. In frustration he finally asked why I was not arguing with his assessment of Christianity. I explained again that if God is as he describes, then we should all come up with good reasons to stay away from Him. If, in fact, God is such a fearful and coldhearted Being, there is every reason in the world not to open the door and let Him in to control our lives. Here again is the great conflict: Many do not want to go to hell at some time in the future, so a Savior of the future appeals to them. However, because of emotional unbelief and fear of what will happen if He is allowed to begin dabbling in their lives, these same people must find some way to cope with life outside of God. This particular man's objections to Christianity had nothing at all to do with intellect; they were purely emotionally motivated.

We know that the stated answers to the test are not descriptive of God, so whom do they describe? Who is it that will not hear us, is not there, and cannot be pleased? Many will answer, "Satan"; others will say, "self." The person I have found most often described in this test is an earthly father. The test taker could be asked the following questions: "Did you fear your father? Did he help you? Was he there? Did he take time out for you? Did he judge you? Could you ever please him, or no matter what you did would he tell you to do more? Did he criticize and require of you what you felt to be the impossible? To this day, do you feel disapproval from him? Did he ever take anything dear from you?" I have found among the defeated whom I disciple that more than ninety percent of the time their concepts of God really describe their fathers (or if not, their mothers or some other influential figures in their lives). All we can know of authority is what we have learned from those in control around us. Does it not then make sense that when we are commanded to call God our Father in heaven, this would stir in our emotions a concept of our father on earth?

There was a girl who had great difficulty praying to or trusting in her Father in heaven; by contrast, she found it quite easy to pray to Jesus, calling Him her Brother. After taking a brief history, it was discovered that at a very early age her father had molested her. She had very naturally transferred her anger and disappointment with her earthly father to her heavenly Father!

When I mentioned to the fellow who was the self-proclaimed intellectual and agnostic that the test he had taken might not describe God but his own father, and we read through the list, the man began to weep. He then told me of his father's leaving and promising to return but never coming back, and of his own hurt and anger as a result of those actions.

If there is one word that describes the condition of the recipients of the Book of Hebrews, it is *unbelief.* They are not able to trust, and the writer battles with their false concept of God derived from interaction with their earthly fathers. "For they disciplined us for a short time as seemed best to them, but He disciplines us for our good, that we may share His holiness" (12:10).

Who, Then, Is God?

I like to read through I Corinthians 13 with those who have an unrealistic concept of God, because if He is love, then this chapter must describe Him. How many sermons have you heard regarding this passage that made you come away thinking, *I have got to love more?* Yet what a joy it is to read it, substituting the name God for the word *love,* and to realize that this is the God who loves us and lives His life through us. God is patient; what a wonderful, most coveted virtue. Patience is not found on our planet; it comes only from heaven. How little patience people exhibit. Ask your mate a question two times in a row (or, if you are daring, three) and see how little patience there is. Many have hearts to help the handicapped, and yet how easily they become discouraged because of the lack of this one attribute. How little patience is found in the Church for those who are growing, even though God is patience. God is kind, not jealous, not a braggart, not arrogant or too proud to be seen with us, He will not act unbecomingly toward us (He will never abuse us), and He never seeks His own but rather what is best for us. That is, any of us under discipline, stress, disease, or physical handicap can be assured that He is allowing it for our good. He is not provoked. Do you know you are never going to make Him so mad that He throws you down to the ground and tramples you? God does not take into account wrongs (He is never keeping a list of offenses as most of us do), hates unrighteousness (any evil that has happened to any of us), will always bear with us, believe in us, endure all things, and will never fail us. He will always be there!

Many have spent their whole lives trying to get their spiritual needs met. Jesus Christ is the only One who can meet those needs, but so often we run from Him because we feel He is something other than the God of I Corinthians 13.

When I had the privilege of sharing with the agnostic about who God really is, and that the man had not been running from Him at all but from a self-made god in the image of his father, he gave his life over to the Lord

Jesus. You see, many people have never given God a fair opportunity to prove Himself, for they reject who they feel He is before He can act on their behalf.

The way out of emotional unbelief is quite simple. We need only confess as sin our wrong feelings of who God is and profess who He really is. It will, however, take time for lying emotions with which we have become so familiar to catch up with the facts. The next failure will test the level of faith to which we have grown. Unbelief is the mother of sin; however, the depth of our unbelief is truly revealed in how we respond to God when we fail. If we wallow, cut ourselves off from Him, and traffic in self-punishment, we reveal the dark depths of unbelief. For in all our self-punishment we prove that we sensed that our acceptance rested not in the Son of God but rather in how well we could perform.

Therefore, next time you fail, do not listen to your lying emotions that say, "God will get you; He will never help you again! He will now make others suffer for your sin." Rather, be a person of faith and believe the God of I Corinthians 13, pressing on in the love and redemption of so great a One. If you have let your lying emotions control you for years, you have a struggle ahead; they do not easily give up the reins to the control of the Spirit.

Remember, I am not saying that we work to change what we are but work to believe what we already are. It will not be easy, for many of us have become accustomed to feeling miserable. We are like the boy who was raised by wolves; when captured by men, he continually fought against those who were trying to help him. He constantly wanted to escape and return to the wet, cold, and harsh existence!

Why? The poor creature had become comfortable with being in a wretched state, and many of us are in a similar condition! We have lived so long cutting ourselves off from God, walking in unbelief, and utilizing our idols that we are more suited to being unhappy—dragging ourselves from one thing to the next looking for contentment—than we would be to say no to our emotions and trust God for who He really is. The choice is ours. If we remain miserable with such a great God, we can blame no one but ourselves!

It is a great step of faith to go against all the lying emotions you have concerning who God is and to open that door to His life one time, for one time is all it will take for you to discover the abundant life for which you have searched so long. There is a verse often quoted to unbelievers which was actually written to unbelieving believers: "Behold, I stand at the door and knock; if anyone hears My voice and opens the door, I will come in to him, and will dine with him, and he with Me" (Revelation 3:20).

CHAPTER 5
FAITH

Many times we seek and do not find because we do not know what finding is. For example, there are those who will never believe God is actually near them throughout the day unless they have a predetermined stirring in their emotions.

When it comes to faith the same is true; many busy themselves trying to find more faith, when they have had all they needed right along. I would like you to think of faith a little differently, as an organ like an ear or eye. When you lie in bed at night, your ears rest but never sleep. If someone starts to break into your house, your ear awakens you in order that you might act! The ear does not create sound but receives it.

Faith is an organ of the Spirit allowing us to receive whatever God is doing. We can readily see why if we have faith as a mustard seed we can move a mountain; the eye of an ant and the eye of a camel both receive light. Faith itself, not quantity of faith, is the issue.

Faith is a wonderful thing, something that every believer possesses. It takes the pressure off us to perform and initiate His works and places emphasis on God, the Creator of the actions. When told by God that his wife was going to have a baby, Abraham immediately looked to himself and said, "I do not think I can father a baby." He looked over at Sarah and said, "I know she cannot have a baby." Then he looked up to God and said, "When are we having the baby?"

CHAPTER 5 | Faith

We have so many promises from God, and those we must learn to greet with the same sequence of responses as Abraham's. We first look to ourselves and know they are impossible. "You are a chosen people, a royal priesthood, a holy nation . . ." (I Peter 2:9). How can it be, Lord? We know it is impossible for us to achieve such stature. Next, we ought to look around us and realize that no other person can help us attain that, either. But then as men and women of faith we look to God and thank Him that it is true; we are a chosen people, a royal priesthood, and a holy nation!

If faith is simply receiving what God desires to do, then do you see how important your concept of God is when it comes to the issues of daily life? Imagine that you are a branch cut off and placed in a vase, dying each day you are there. No matter how hard you work and strain, the leaves and petals continue to fall off; you simply have no life within you. Just before you die, you are taken out and grafted into a vine that possesses all the life you need. But what if you believe that the life that will be coming from the vine is poisoned and will bring your vulnerable existence to an immediate end? What will you do? You will try everything you can to keep that life out of you, even as you continue to die.

The same is true in our spiritual lives; many have a concept of God that is poisoned. They do not know who He is, and even though they are dying, they refuse to allow His life to enter in.

The Hard Part

Just as the Spirit drove Jesus into the wilderness to be tempted, He sometimes will drive us into a wilderness to have our faith tested.

64 | SIDETRACKED IN THE WILDERNESS

Imagine walking into a room when the Lord Himself steps in behind you, turns out the lights, closes and locks the door, and then completely removes from you the awareness of His nearness, emotional responses to Him, and the consciousness that He hears you! You set out to work as hard as you can to regain these; there is, however, one major complexity. As long as you work to experience His presence, you extend your time in the darkened room, because its purpose is to teach you to walk by faith, not by sight or feeling.

Oh, yes, there is one other thing. When you have tried almost everything to regain emotional awareness, the enemy slips in and says things like, "If only you had not done such and such, God would be near to you." "If only you had moved to such and such a place, He would be with you now." "If only you had married another person, everything would be much better." "If only you had not failed the Lord, He would be pleased to be near you now." "If only you had prayed more and memorized more Scriptures, you would sense the Lord's presence."

In the midst of this you might even doubt whether you are truly born again; you will ask anew that the Lord Jesus come into your life; you will seek for signs or anything that will give the assurance so desperately needed. You repent of every imaginable sin and punish yourself with the most severe forms of guilt. You want to perform in order to get God's acceptance.

Many who boast of breathtaking faith, telling magnificent stories of all that they have accomplished because of their awesome belief, are crushed and dismantled in this room, and why not? How long can a man who trusts in himself walk in darkness and not stumble and be overcome, broken, and humbled? Yes, here you walk in absolute darkness, one that can even be felt (Exodus 10:21, 22). This type of darkness Job knew all too well: "My face is flushed from weeping, and deep darkness is on my eyelids" (16:16). "He has walled up my way so that I cannot pass; and He has put darkness on my paths" (19:8). ". . . when I waited for light then darkness came" (30:26).

This prolonged state of darkness will test us and reveal any unbelief that might reside within. The longer the period of darkness and absence of emotion, the more will be revealed. We will again try a series of procedures to regain our emotional standing, all of which will be telling of what we really trust in our daily lives to bring contentment, and which God, of course, will not allow to succeed. It may be revealed that we trust idols, those things in which we find some measure of comfort (Isaiah 42:17). Perhaps we trust in particular brothers or sisters who, we are sure, can get us out of our present calamity (Jeremiah 9:4; Micah 7:5), and yet we find that they have no answers. We may look again to the teaching that promised us eternal bliss, that one doctrine that brought a promised experience, and we will return to it with all the more zeal, but alas, we still walk in darkness and may now believe that we were deceived (Jeremiah 28:15). We might appeal to our achievements and the many things done in the past, hoping that God will recognize our great value and return (Jeremiah 48:7). It may even be revealed that we have trusted in fame to continue living the abundant life (Ezekiel 16:14).

When everything fails, we begin to complain, making the error that so many do: In the midst of misfortune we do not simply remain silent and wait, but instead begin to blame God for the whole situation. We, like Job, begin to curse the day we were made and even accuse Him of the grave mistake of making us. We can go so far as to become angry with God, charging Him with not caring and doing nothing. "You have said, 'It is vain to serve God; and what profit is it that we have kept His charge, and that we have walked in mourning before the Lord of hosts?'" (Malachi 3:14)

We become sick of the whole situation. Blind, irrational, and void of hope, it becomes impossible any longer to see God's hand in this process. We must have our eyes opened.

As Paul writes the letter of Philemon, he makes it clear that he is in prison, probably in Rome. True to custom there, he was no doubt chained to a guard, and as he wrote the letter he would hear the clanging of the chains and see the guard, constant reminders of his condition of bondage. Yet Paul mentioned three times that he was a prisoner of Jesus Christ and the Gospel. What is the significance of these statements, given Paul's situation? He did not see a Roman guard at the end of his chain but instead saw Jesus Christ! The man of faith never sees bondage to anything but God Himself. You see, nothing comes into our lives without first passing through the loving hands of our Father in heaven.

What do you see at the end of the chain that binds you? Do you see your mate, your job, your sin, your failures, your circumstance? Instead, would you be willing to see Jesus Christ as the Author of it, which will allow you to rest, knowing that the outcome will be for your ultimate benefit?

I had been a Christian for only a few months when I decided to attend a conference in a large city. I spent each afternoon downtown, witnessing to whomever I met. As I rounded a corner, more than two blocks away was a man who turned and began to walk in my direction. As he came closer, I sensed the Lord telling me, "Give the man all of your money!" I had $150, which at that time was a considerable amount. As the man passed by, I stopped him and began to witness to him. To my amazement, he promptly began to witness to me of God's love and faithfulness; I barely got a word in. Finally, the brother told me that he must get going and asked that I pray for him. I said, "Brother, what am I to pray for?"

He responded, "I have been out of work for two months and cannot find a job. I have a wife and two children, and we are out of food, but I have learned that God is faithful and will provide." I was amazed at his faith. Then I reached into my pocket, handed him the $150, and told him the Lord had told me to give this to him when I first saw him. The brother grabbed me and held me, beginning to weep and praise the Lord. I walked away feeling that "my heart was as light as my pocket," as Hudson Taylor once said after giving all that he had to the Lord. I was so amazed that God knew exactly when we both would be walking down this street, and He orchestrated a meeting at the perfect time to reward the brother's faith.

On another occasion a brother who had lost his job came to me. I told him I was concerned over his loss and asked how he was doing. He said that he really was not worried, for he had enough savings to last six months. As I walked away, I remarked to my wife, "He would be much better off if he only had one month's savings, for now he will have to wait six months before the Lord gives him a job." You see, he would have to lose his savings, that which he was trusting, before he could enter into true faith and trust in God as Provider!

Who is like our God, His lessons so wonderful, so perfectly fitted to our condition and His purpose? We must all take this course on faith, for without it we cannot please God. The exact nature of each believer's course will differ, being tailor-made by a loving Father, but the results will always be the same. "For momentary, light affliction is producing for us an eternal weight of glory far beyond all comparison" (II Corinthians 4:17).

One last thought: The greatness of faith is not to be judged by how many of God's promises you have experienced today, or how much material gain you possess, or even how much good health you have received. The greatness of your faith is shown in proportion to how long you can wait for the fulfillment of a promise. Again, greatness of faith is not proven in what is received, but in how long a person can wait without wavering to receive.

What would you think of a farmer who planted his wheat and the following day was running up and down his field with a harvester? You would consider the farmer to be quite mad, of course, because he had not learned to wait for God to do His life-sustaining transformation under the ground, out of sight of man.

So it is with the promises of God. We must wait, and the greatness of faith is proven in the ability of the believer to rest until harvest, knowing all the while that the work that must be done is a supernatural one that God alone can accomplish.

We must also come to see that it is rarely in the big events that true faith is shown or proven. I have known people who have endured great persecution and imprisonment because of their commitment to Christ, and yet they could not deny themselves in the little things of life. It is easier to lay down one's physical life than it is to lay down self-life, but great faith is shown in the small, insignificant things of life.

Once we have completed our lesson on faith, we will be much more ready to accept without question everything that God tells us. We will be better equipped no longer to trust in our idols, in what we feel, or even in what we see; we will understand we are to trust only in Him. His answers concerning the freedom from self, sin, and the world will not be wasted, for we will drink in each answer with the quiet confidence and fullness of a faith that hopes in God alone. We will know that the fulfillment of our hope is no greater than the promise.

CHAPTER 6

The Conviction of Self-life

"If anyone wishes to come after Me, let him deny himself, and take up his cross daily, and follow Me. For whoever wishes to save his life shall lose it, but whoever loses his life for My sake, he is the one who will save it" (Luke 9:23, 24). Jesus says the way to life will be through death, and if we are to follow Him, we must deny self. What is this self that we are commanded to deny, and what is the life that must be lost in order to live?

The Development of Self-life

According to I John 4:8, God is love. Since love must have an object, God created man to be this entity. To assure that His inclination to love would be met, God put in man's spirit the need to be loved and accepted by Him. The moment we are born, we are driven to find our Creator to meet this need within us.

There is, however, one major obstacle to having God meet our spiritual need for love and acceptance. We are born dead to God in our spirits, making it impossible to have the desire fulfilled. In Genesis 2:17, God said, "But from the tree of the knowledge of good and evil you shall not eat, for in the day that you eat from it you shall surely die." It was an absolute imperative that if Adam and Eve ate of the tree they would die! They did eat thereof, and God said they were dead, even though their souls were still active (they were thinking, feeling, and choosing) and their bodies were still functioning. They were dead and yet living;

where, then, did the death take place? There is only one place left—the spirit. They were dead to God in the spirit, the result being that it would now be impossible to have met their deepest needs of spiritual love and acceptance that could come only from God. This condition presents three particular problems for man.

The Inescapable Emptiness

First, being created for the express purpose of receiving love and acceptance from God, and yet as a result of spiritual death dealing with the impossibility of getting the need met, man is driven to make up for this deficiency. The ambition to have this need met is so great that it consumes man's energies, making all else inconsequential in comparison to the longing. In short, all that matters is getting his needs met. Man becomes thoroughly and intensely self-centered in his quest for love and acceptance, and he ends up looking in places other than to God.

A Christian woman I was discipling confessed to numerous affairs in the span of one month. I asked her why she was doing such a thing; was it because she enjoyed sex so much? No, not at all; in fact, she disliked sex. She disclosed that she simply wanted someone to tell her that they loved and wanted her, even if they were drunk and lying. For her, sex was a religion in the sense that it was being used to attempt to meet her deep inner needs.

The self-centered life is a miserable one. It tries to draw every item in the world to itself, but after once being sampled each article is tossed aside as the search continues for that something that will meet the need. It does not matter if the items it takes in are animate or inanimate; they all become castaways. Never mind if it is parents, a mate, children, or friends; all will be disposed of or judged irrelevant if they are unable to satisfy the inner thirst. Career, possessions, alcohol, status, the self-centered person must sample everything he can until the perfect religion, that one recipe that will bring satiation to inherent want, is found.

Consider the stupidity of self-centered life. It would appear that the zenith of God's creation—man—possesses no powers of observation whatsoever to judge the outcome of this existence. Does man show no evidence of reason? Are those who change mates as easily as if they were getting a new pair of shoes really happy? Is the woman really more content now that she is in total charge of the home? Is the homosexual really pleased having confessed to his alternative lifestyle? Does the woman feel satisfied knowing she has preserved her "human rights" by putting to death an unborn child? If we could regain rationality, we would conclude that the self-centered life comprises emptiness, weariness, and misery, with the blind leading the blind. Unfortunately, self-life is a force much greater than reason, capable of enslaving mankind.

If a husband and wife both refuse to lose an argument or give up a single right, choosing conflict over harmony, should it surprise anyone that neighbors cannot get along? And if neighbors are protecting their rights in disregard of others, would it then shock anyone to see that nations go to war? Self-life is ugly, wicked, and will always lead to misery, controlling people and giving them a truly beastly existence. That is what it means to be carnal, to live as an animal.

An animal has a soul (mind, will, emotions) and a body, but no spirit. Each year our dog has puppies; when they are ready to be weaned, the mother will go to my wife and bark, signaling that it is time for my wife to begin some of the feeding. It all sounds very noble, the mother appealing to my wife for help, and I am quite certain that the dog is concerned about the state of her offspring. However, when my wife takes the food to the puppies, the mother dog is overwhelmed by her own animal instincts (self-life) and pushes away the very puppies she wanted nourished, eating the food herself. In that moment all good judgment leaves, and she proves herself not a conscientious mother, but just an animal.

How often this same type of thing is seen today in parents; when they lie in bed at night or are driving by themselves down a road, their minds are filled with love for their children. Oh, how they want to do what is good for each child; how blessed they feel to have young ones! They resolve to do more for and with their children, beginning tomorrow. But, alas, when tomorrow comes, self-life is still in control, and each child's needs must give way to the activities of the parents, who would rather drink, watch television, stay late at work, or converse with adults.

In my work I am amazed at the depth and extent of the hideous nature of the self-life; I often see whole families destroyed because a self-centered husband believes that a woman ten years younger than his wife will surely meet his need. The destruction and sacrifice of the very lives of his own children mean nothing; they are not even considered when compared with the possibility of fulfilling his own desires.

I once asked a woman whose husband was living in adultery to explain to me why she wanted him to return.

Was it because she feared what might be the punishment for a cheating Christian? Was it because of the impact that a divorce might have on the children? Or was it because she was miserable and wanted to be happy once again? What do you think her answer was? Of course, so she could be happy again! It had nothing to do with his wellbeing or that of the children!

There are certain characteristics that the self-centered possess. For example, they always want to be seen, to be the center of attention, and to draw adulation to their accomplishments. They cannot bear to be criticized or appear to be inferior. They manipulate, distort the meaning of the actions of others, and often lie. They are overly sensitive, always comparing themselves to others, and hold to trifling opinions. Be careful, for they will always seek revenge, are easily irritated, refuse blame, and lust after those things that are forbidden. They manifest abrasiveness, intimidation, arrogance, and pride. They are boastful, compulsive, vain, critical, dominant, guilty, insecure, preachy, self-absorbed, slow to forgive, and unteachable. Also, when hearing a list like this, they always think of someone else they wish would read it and be convicted.

How did man find himself in such a condition? It began when Adam sinned and fell out of the heavenly life of fellowship with God into the life of the world. He attempted to meet his ethereal need here on earth through a life of self-pleasing. The self-centered man is blinded both to his condition and to the destruction that he causes, not only in his own life but also in its wake. He will begin to experience turmoil in the personality, disturbed emotions, and sickness, followed by discord and division in his relationships with others.

The Search for Sanity

I would like you to think of your mind, will, and emotions as an automobile and the spirit as the driver. Automobiles are created for drivers; if there were no drivers there would most certainly be no need for automobiles. Now imagine that you are standing at the bottom of a hill and you notice that a car is careening down toward you with no driver in it! What will you do? I would guess that you will do your best to get out of the way of the runaway auto. Why? Because it has no driver and is therefore out of control. What if the car continued in a straight line; would you still get out of its way? If it began to weave, would you nevertheless remove yourself from its path? Suppose the car began to roll toward you, would you move away just the same? The answer to all three questions is yes, of course. My point is that there are varying degrees of being out of control; in fact, sometimes the car may even appear to be restrained, but you know that it is not and, because of that, refuse to trust it.

I define sanity as having one's mind, will, and emotions under the control of the Holy Spirit. Technically, sanity is being in touch with reality, and what can be more real than being in touch with God? Therefore, if we are all born dead to God in the spirit, what is every man's condition at birth? Insanity! Insanity is merely being out of touch with reality, and God is the only absolute reality. Many will find this thought repulsive, because they, like the automobile that is moving in a straight line, do not like to be classified with the more overtly out-of-control autos that crash and burn much sooner. But both are in the same condition in varying degrees. Even the believer who is born again and has Christ's Spirit within his renewed inner person can erect a wall of unbelief that disallows Christ's rule over the soul; at that moment the believer, too, is quite insane.

Many writing on spiritual warfare and the ploys of Satan have noted that he makes his voice sound just like a person's own. His purpose in doing this is to make humans believe that the thoughts originate within themselves and are their own actual desires. Let me illustrate: Satan would not walk right up to a man and say, "Leave your wife for a younger woman." Instead, he has access to the man's thoughts and says, "I think I should leave my wife." This is all calculated to confuse the issue, since the enemy would like us to believe that any temptation is, in fact, our own desire. Once he has accomplished that deception, every time we say no to an allurement we believe we are saying no to what we really want. We may then dwell on it until we embrace it as our own and no longer are willing to withstand it. This will give rise to sin. "But each one is tempted when he is carried away and enticed by his own lust. Then when lust has conceived, it gives birth to sin; and when sin is accomplished, it brings forth death" (James 1:14, 15).

Does temptation equal desire? If that were true, then the wickedest man ever to walk on the face of the earth was Jesus Christ, who was tempted in all things! "For we do not have a high priest who cannot sympathize with our weaknesses, but one who has been tempted in all things as we are, yet without sin" (Hebrews 4:15). Yet, we find Christians who always confess their temptations as sin.

I explained this principle to my wife, who agreed. Then I asked her if she had ever been tempted to commit adultery. She seemed offended as she said, "What kind of woman do you think I am?" I noted that her response proved that she still believed that temptation equaled desire. Although the enemy can put absolutely any thought into our minds at nearly any time, these do not represent our wishes, but rather his true character.

A friend once told me that there are only two types of people who have anything to do with sheep: butchers and shepherds. He explained that the butcher's voice, though it may sound like one's own, will always be hurtful, harsh, condemning, critical, depressing, confusing, and above all else, driving. If not dealt with, it will persist until the one spoken to believes he is hearing his individual predisposition. On the other hand, the Shepherd's voice is gentle, loving, and teaching; it leads, lifts the spirit (even when convicting), and brings life and freedom. I have found this simple test of the voices that I hear to be quite useful.

One day while I was sharing with a woman, the Holy Spirit brought her to the certainty that she wanted to receive Christ into her life. After she prayed and asked the Lord to enter in, I suggested that she bow her head, shut everything out, look within where Christ was now dwelling, listen for His voice, and then tell me what He told her. Before long there was a wide smile on her face; He had told her that she was acceptable to Him and that He loved her. No sooner had she gotten the words out of her mouth than her countenance changed and she began to cry. I told her to stop right there. I said, "This is what you just heard: 'I must work to please God, but I know that I will fail Him, and soon He will be displeased with me.'" She looked astonished and affirmed my statement. I then told her that it was not so! The truth was that she was pleasing to God already, and she was to work not for His favor, but because she already had it. I explained about the voice of the Shepherd that she first heard and the voice of the butcher; she could readily tell the difference between the two. I was happy that she had only been a believer for a few minutes and had distinguished between the two, something that many who have been believers for years have yet to discern.

If we have not learned to judge the source of our thoughts, it will go without saying that we are not judging our emotions, which are much more deceiving and useful to the enemy. One problem is that emotions feel the same whether their source is truth or falsehood.

For example, guilt feels the same whether it is the outcome of real events or not. In a fit of anger, a man once hit another in the head with a brick; assuming that he had killed the man, he fled to another country, where he died a guilt-ridden alcoholic. At the time of the man's funeral, the fellow who had been assumed murdered was in the area and decided to attend to show that there were no hard feelings. The first man suffered his life away under the false guilt of being a murderer, and even though he was not, the feelings remained.

Emotions are deceptive. If someone feels worthless, many may try to convince him that he is not, but he will still walk through life feeling worthless. The unsupervised emotions of man provide quite a playground for Satan; there he can maximize his calculated destruction with minimum effort.

I know from experience that after one traffics in depression for a period of time, it can come to be the normal course of the day. When I first began to understand lying emotions, I realized that I could be sitting down doing my work when all of a sudden I would be depressed. There was never any center to the depression; it just simply appeared. Since I was not aware at that time that feelings can wander, I would not call them back, the result being that I would be in the doldrums for several days. When the Lord did reveal what was happening, He also showed me that just as it would be ridiculous to stay for days wherever my wandering thoughts might take me, it was equally ludicrous to spend time where my lying emotions were taking me. Just as we can judge thoughts and reject them, we also can determine which emotions are following the enemy's lead.

We were not created to live independently of Him; that brings insanity. It is only in humble dependence upon the Creator that mind and emotions enter into soundness and trustworthiness. Being born dead to God in the spirit has caused us to be self-centered in our attempts to have our deepest needs met; it also has caused us to exist in a condition of insanity, wherein we have listened to and acted upon false thoughts and lying emotions.

The final result of being born dead to God in the spirit is loss of identity; we were created for God, and yet we are not brought into the world possessed by Him, or Him by us. Therefore, our very reason for existence is not apparent. We are born in a condition of not knowing who we are but being driven to find out. What happens next is really quite incredible. In our self-centered, insane conditions we ask other self-centered, insane people, "Would you please tell me who I am?" Can you imagine going into a mental institution and interviewing the residents to find out who you really are? What would be even more amazing is if someone told you that you were Napoleon and you believed him, thanked him, and left, adopting your new identity. Yet this is exactly what mankind has done. Being born without God, self-centered and insane, we have received identity messages from others in the same condition and proceeded to believe and live out of them!

Our Controlling Identity

Much has been written on the topic of identity and its effects. Here is a simple illustration that will help show how identity is affecting each person.

Think about the impression that you would like to leave after you exit a room full of people. What do you hope will be said about you? You might desire to project some of the following attributes: caring, kind, helpful, a good spouse and parent, intelligent, successful, attractive, and spiritual. If I were to auction off such a person as these words describe, how much money would I collect? Probably quite a bit, because the one word that sums up this person is *worth*. This person has great value.

Now write a description of yourself at your very worst moment. Remember, what you are at your worst moment is your true condition! When nothing has gone right (your child is sick, problems are arising in interpersonal relationships, someone is attacking your character, a great embarrassment has occurred, you have failed the Lord, finances are lacking), how would you describe yourself? Would you use such terms as angry, vindictive, a slanderer, a failure, a phony, carnal, stupid, ugly, depressed, and a terrible parent and mate? Or in your worst moments do you become proud, arrogant, self-reliant, and withdrawn from the support of others? If I took this person to the auction, how much money would I receive? This one would probably return home unsold, for no one would want someone so worthless. Would you want to be married to the person described above? Would you want him as your parent? How would you like to have him working for you?

Because we are all the things that we described at our worst moment, it becomes evident that no one will accept or love us. This realization creates considerable discomfort, since acceptance and love are our deepest needs. Therefore, in order to milk love and acceptance out of others, we run to an imaginary sewing machine to make a "success suit" that looks exactly like the impression we hope to make on others, put the suit on, and button it to the top so no one can see what is really under it. Our relationships with people are somewhat stressed; on the one hand, we ask them to come near and give us love and acceptance on the merits of our success suits, and yet on the other hand we push them away for fear that if they get too close, they may see and reject the real person covered up.

Suppose I could persuade you that you are a rabbit! How long could you hop? Five, ten minutes, maybe fifteen? After you had hopped so long, what would you be ready to do? Stand up, of course! Your whole body would begin to ache from jumping and attempting to be what you are not. When you are living in your success suit, you are merely hopping. You feel you must, of course, for who would accept the real you? So you get up at 7:00 a.m., put on your success suit, and begin to hop! By 6:00 p.m. what are you ready to do? Stand up, rip off that uncomfortable suit that has been suffocating you, and be what you really are! Therefore, the world has the benefit of knowing you in your success suit while you hop, but your family reaps the consequences of knowing the real you.

A certain Christian businessman was addicted to pornography. He would be sitting in his office when the thought would enter his mind, *I think I will go to the porno store tonight.* At that the struggle would begin: *No, I will not go; I am a Christian! I will not go!* In the evening when he got in his car, he would repeat, *I will not go,* as he drove to the porno store. He would stop in the parking lot, *But I will not go in.* Standing outside the door, the inner argument would continue: *I will not go in.* In he would go, thinking, *I will not stay.* Once he picked up a magazine, the struggle was over. You see, his assumed identity—what he believed he really was—was that of a degenerate hypocrite, and all of his refusals were mere hopping.

One proof that what we are at our worst moments is our true condition is that we have tried to cover it up with the success suit. Another proof is that people can control us through this identity. For example, a man is attracted to a woman because she continues to affirm that his success suit is the real him. He is manipulated and contorted through all of her positive statements that allow him—even if just briefly—to believe the lie that he is something different from what he feels. So the man marries the woman, and after a few months of marriage she realizes that she can also control him by hinting that his true identity is what he fears he is at his worst. He is now being controlled by negative statements. However, at the same time his secretary at work is telling him how wonderful his success suit is. Who would the man rather be with? Perhaps he leaves his wife and marries the secretary, and after a few months she begins to control through confirming what he is afraid he is; but never fear, a new secretary is lauding his success suit, and so the cycle continues.

If he did not believe that what he is at his worst moment is his true condition, he would not be upset and angry when someone hints at that being the case. How a person responds to negative evaluation is a sure test of who he believes he is. If when told he is a failure someone reacts in anger, it is because he believes that he is a failure. People in the business of covering up their true identities hang on every word and event and manifest great hostility when anything confirms their fear of who they really are.

The Molding of Self-life

Past events affect most areas of life. The attitude of a person approaching his boss depends on past experience. Certain behavior is expected from a mate when one returns home at night. We draw upon the past continually, and it will help us to understand the self that must be denied to realize that identity messages of the past do have great significance today.

We have all received a variety of identity messages. Some are quite obvious, while others speak just as loudly without utilizing words. For example, I might say to you that I do not like you; that would be easily comprehended. On the other hand, while you are talking to me I may simply walk off, saying nothing. In both instances I was able to communicate to you how I felt. As you are given these messages, not only do you have lying emotions and thoughts to contend with, but also the enemy, who will take every message and distort it in order that you might receive it as having the worst possible intent.

Many parents have been accused of giving their children negative identity messages that were never intended. The enemy has merely seized the opportunity and, in the voice that sounds like the parents' own, told them something other than what was meant. For instance, a girl may remember her father pushing her off his lap and, ten years later, say that is when she realized her father no longer loved her. Yet the reason the father did it may have been so he could go to work. The enemy used the situation to tell the girl a lie, which she believed.

There is also a person's peculiar grid of emotions to contend with, which I envision as a screen door that exists between that individual and the rest of the world. When something is said, it hits this screen of emotion and takes a flip, causing the person to hear what might not have been said at all.

A woman once told me that when she was thirteen her mother died, and so it fell upon her to cook and care for her father and two younger brothers. Every night she would try her best to cook a perfect meal for her father, but without exception he would find something wrong with the meal and end his observation with, "You'll never be a good wife if you don't learn how to cook." The girl grew up continually hearing this same statement. At age twenty she married, and three months later she decided to surprise her husband with some fresh biscuits. He took one bite and made the objective remark that they needed a little more sugar. At that the woman stomped out of the house, saying she was leaving for good and he could find a wife that could cook! The husband stood there dumbfounded, staring at the half-eaten biscuit and thinking, *I should've eaten it just like it was!* All he said was that the biscuits needed more sugar, but what did she hear? "You'll never be a good wife if you don't learn how to cook."

So often this is what happens when we respond through the grid of emotion that has been patterned by messages received and which continues to confirm what we are feeling. On a scale of one to ten, what is a ten in importance to us may only be a one for others. Once an identity is developed, we will begin to look for signals that verify it. For example, if a friend and I are told by our boss that we are stupid, and I possess a positive identity, that may tell me that it is really the boss who is mentally deficient. On the other hand, if my friend feels, due to past messages, that he lacks intelligence, what the boss said validates his worst fear that he truly is stupid.

A child who receives the idea that he is not valuable may test this hypothesis by rebelling and staying out all night. Under these circumstances, if the parents say nothing, or worse yet, say it would be better had the child not been born, this one will believe what he always suspected was true. This can result in further defiance and even open doors for the enemy to tempt in the area of suicide, for the child is convinced that he has no worth.

Identity Messages Given

Many children receive from parents the communication that they are not needed or wanted, such as when, for instance, the parents decide to divorce. The child cannot understand the complexities of the divorce; he can only assume the obvious: "It is not important to Dad that he be with me." A message of worth is given to the child as he observes what it is to which the parents give their time. If when the phone rings the father drops everything and answers it, then the person on the phone must have value. However, if Dad never takes time to talk to the child, the little one can only conclude that he does not have importance. If the mother is working to support the family, that is one thing, but if she is working to buy more material objects and to get away from the kids, that is quite another issue. The children who have had to sacrifice time with parents who pursued material gain will often despise and refuse to take care of those purchased objects. Why? Material goods are seen as competitors for the parents' attention.

Similarly, a wife may like the woman down the street until she finds out that her husband is having an affair with her; at that point she will find a variety of things wrong with the woman. The same is true of a husband's habits of watching television, reading the paper, or working, activities with which a wife finds nothing wrong until these begin to steal the attentions that she should be receiving. She reacts to the message that other pursuits are more important than she is.

There are two things that can greatly affect a woman's identity: One is if her father at some point in time stopped hugging her and showing affection, and the other is if she was molested. In either case, the message was given that she was not loved. There are many women who have a ten-, twenty-, or even thirty-year-old need to be loved by their fathers. Withholding proper affection sends a strong message.

There is, unfortunately, around the world great discrimination derived from appearance. While I was in India in a small village, a woman came to me with pockmarked face, crooked teeth, a slight frame, and one foot that bent in. She would not even look me in the face as she handed me a piece of paper on which she had listed how she would cope with life. You see, she had been told she was a curse to the family, they would never be able to find her a husband, and she would always be a burden. On that small piece of paper she had scribbled that she would go in and out the back door and only do housework at night so no one else in the family would have to see her. She said that she would like to commit suicide, but did not have the nerve, and therefore would eagerly await natural death. What was this poor lady's identity? Only because of appearance was she rejected, and many in every country have received the same treatment. As I looked at the woman, the Holy Spirit spoke to me: "It is for her, and her alone, that I have sent you to India." Could it be that eight weeks on the road, sleepless nights, near exhaustion, homesickness, and speaking day after day were all for this one person? I said, "If you are so worthless, why did the Lord just reveal to me that I was brought all the way from the United States only to meet you?" I love the way He works, which is not according to man's thoughts or plans! This Hindu girl gave her life to Christ that very moment. It must be true that every hair on our heads is numbered, and even the weakest and feeblest among us are watched over by the Lord, who hears our cries of distress.

A child can receive identity messages from the parent who does too little or too much. If the father never helps with a child's projects, he is saying the child is not worthy of his time. If, on the other hand, every time the young one works on a project the father takes the screwdriver out of his hand to "do it right," the child is being told that he is incompetent. If a daughter must make her bed, but repeatedly finds mother in the room remaking it, soon the daughter will believe she cannot do things right.

While I was a campus minister I often noticed students whose parents had done everything for them; when they arrived on campus they had no skills with which to make decisions. The end result was that some very poor choices were made, for they would procrastinate when faced with alternatives until impulsively forced to resolve the matter. Since most hasty decisions have negative outcomes, this prompted the students to wait even longer before choosing a course the next time, and thus emerged an ever-tightening spiral of bad decision-making.

I have often suggested to parents that when their child comes to them with a request (such as, "Can I spend the night at a friend's house?"), they should say no if they do not want the child to do the thing, but if they do not care, they should have the child make the decision and give reasons for the choice. I have been surprised at the times my children did not go somewhere when it was their decision; they would have gone immediately had I said yes. When we feel that we must control everything our children do, we can leave them with the silent message that they are too stupid to make a decision.

A loud message is always delivered when parents talk about the son or daughter who is such a great success in terms of position, achievement, wealth, and so on. The point of triumph for the rest of the children becomes similar accomplishment. Anything less is failure, about which they are reminded every time the eminent child is acclaimed.

These are just a few of the messages that we receive in our insane conditions. As you can well suppose, there are countless more, as varied as are those who must absorb them. Once the messages are received and believed, the identity of what we are at our worst begins to be molded. It may include feelings of worthlessness, inferiority, depression, not being wanted, stupidity, failure, ugliness, guilt, and self-hatred. Then every mistake begins to prove to us that not only do we feel this way about ourselves, but it is actually what we are.

The attempts (success suits) to cover identity take on many forms, including such things as titles, professions, church work, dress, possessions, being an ideal parent or spouse, intellectualism, self-abasement (yes, one can glory in this), talents, or supporting particular social or political stands. All are efforts to keep hidden what we fear is true. In short, we hate ourselves! Frustration in life will come from any events that prove we are the very things we have tried so hard not to be. The use of idols is merely an extension of that dark, hated thing called self-life. All attempts to deny it have failed. How to be free is the question.

The Problem Is Not The Problem

Keeping in mind the two identities previously discussed, the success suit and the one arising from worst moments, I would like you to envision three circles, one placed after the other in a row. In the first circle on the far left I would like you to put that one problem or sin that continues to overwhelm and defeat you time and time again. We will call this first circle the Problem Circle. I will, for the sake of illustration, place the problem of alcohol in this circle. We can work up a variety of approaches for overcoming alcohol: making it illegal, giving drugs that make those who drink ill, even locking up the people with the problem where it would be impossible to get a drink. We can be thankful to any organization that helps people stop drinking, for the destruction of families because of the addiction is tremendous. However, one problem is that many times there is a man who has an identity that is a mess, and he is an alcoholic. He is, in fact, a drunken mess. There are two ways to be controlled by alcohol: One is by having to get it, and the other is by needing to stay away from it. In either case, the alcohol must become the focus of a person's life. When the problem is seen as alcohol only, and the man stops drinking, he becomes a sober mess. The problem is not the problem.

Let us now move to the center circle, which we will call the Event Circle. What has taken place to cause this person to begin to drink? It may be a very insignificant event; however, something has occurred that caused this person to become angry and rebellious. In order to have a problem we must rebel against God, and the only thing that will justify rebellion is anger.

Let me illustrate. A teenager asks his mother if he can go to an all-night party, and the mother refuses. The boy then commences to pick a fight with his mother until she says something that makes him angry, at which time he stomps off to the party, feeling perfectly justified in his rebellion. The next morning the mother asks, "Why did you go against my wishes?"

The boy responds, "Because you made me mad." You see, now it is her fault that he rebelled. If you are on the receiving end of this type of behavior, it is no fun whatsoever.

Suppose a man has decided to commit adultery with someone at work. He knows that such an act is not good for his marriage, his children, or the office. He cannot justify the behavior. Therefore, he goes home and picks a fight with his wife until she says something that offends him, and in his anger he feels perfectly justified in driving to the other woman's house. The greater the rebellion in our lives, the more hostility we must generate to feel good about it.

So it is with the Christian who is rebelling against God. He must bring himself to a point of anger before he can justify his rebellion, and the greater the rebellion the greater the need for anger.

With this in mind, let us ask again what the event was that caused the drinking problem. This person and two others were taken into the boss's office and scolded for not producing enough at work. As the man thought about this throughout the day, he became angry and found himself drunk that evening. So we might say that the event is the real problem, and in order to solve the resulting difficulty with excessive drinking, the man should leave his job and find a new one, thereby changing his circumstances. But, we must ask, why is it that Jim and Ed were called into the boss's office with this man to receive the same reprimand, and yet they did not get drunk that evening? What is the difference between these men and their co-worker?

We now move to the third circle, which we will label Identity. There is something in this man's identity not found in Jim's or Ed's that allows particular events to control him. If we would place in this circle what this man believes he is at his worst moments, we would notice that whenever an occurrence seems to attest to this, the man will become angry, rebel, and cope by turning to one of his old idols from the past. That is, whenever an experience undresses him by removing his success suit, the man will become angry and drink.

Imagine that you came to my office, and as you left I informed you that you must leave all your clothes with me. You have no choice; you must travel home completely naked. I presume that would put you under considerable stress. How might you cope with the pressure of going all the way home naked? You could get drunk and lose your inhibitions, or opt to take drugs and enjoy ridding yourself of the confines of clothing. You might become depressed and say, "Well, I never deserved clothes anyway." Perhaps you would hide behind every bush to withdraw from the eyes of others, or yell and scream, causing others to run from you and thus not see you. My point is that whenever an event takes place that proves you are the very thing you have worked so hard not to be, you will become angry, rebel, and develop some way of coping with the nakedness you sense from having your success suit removed. We can conclude that the problem is not the problem, the event is not the problem, but your identity at your worst is the problem.

This principle is often operating in the marriage relationship. Many have never really fallen in love, which is the desire to do good for someone else. On the contrary, they have fallen in lust with the outer life of the mate. After a short term of marriage, because the success suit has worn off, the husband or wife will begin to tear away at the mate's inner life, finding it quite disgusting, and yet at the same time expect the spouse, after such an emotional beating, to give his or her outer life to sex without reservation. A marriage partner wants us to love his or her whole person, which, depending on the amount of past damage done to the inner life, may be quite impossible. Some have inner lives that are truly unlovable; they know it, and if we confirm it to them we must pay a price: They will withdraw or explode to punish us for our observations. Remember that God does possess an answer for every such dilemma.

I would like you to imagine two cups that represent two different individuals, boys A and B. Both cups are the same size and hold a specific amount of water, but rather than fill these cups with water, we will be filling them with stress. When these cups are full and more gets added, they will simply spill over. Boy A begins his life at an adoption agency, and therefore is feeling unwanted, which causes his cup to be fifty percent full of stress. Boy B, however, has had very little happen in his life to cause him any distress. Their first-grade teacher could not tell any difference in the amount of anxiety that the two boys had, because neither of them had reached 100 percent yet. In high school, boys A and B are told by their respective girlfriends that they are going to date other boys. That causes Boy B's pressure level to go up to five percent; however, because Boy A is already feeling unwanted at fifty percent, what is a five percent event for Boy B is a twenty percent event for Boy A, and his tension goes to seventy percent. Both boys decide to get married after completing school. Marriage adds 25 percent stress to anyone's life no matter how well adjusted he is; therefore, Boy B goes to thirty percent stress, but Boy A goes to 95 percent. Someone just ran out of room to handle much difficulty!

Life is full of six-percent events, which are not constant, but come and go. These include such things as running out of gas, spilling a drink, the children's breaking the lawn mower, the neighbor's complaining about the dog, or a person's desk being moved at work. Suppose that I am standing on my front porch drinking a cup of coffee and notice that the garage doors to the houses of boys A and B are opening at the same time. I can see that both boys' cars have flat tires—a six-percent event for each—and their responses are completely different! Boy A begins to shout, scream, curse, blame his wife for not checking the air in the tires, and beat the car with the tire wrench. Boy B begins to whistle and decides that it might be fun to get his hands dirty; he is grateful that his wife was not driving the car when the puncture occurred. The problem is not the flat tire, but the amount of stress carried over from the past and the acquired disposition from it.

The deception that many people have is that the six-percent event is the real problem. If my husband treated me better, if I had a better job, if the kids behaved, if my parents would apologize, if I owned a new car, then all would be well! But these are, as we mentioned before, only the branches that reveal root rot, which is the inner life that has taken on an identity which it hates, which controls, and which must remain hidden from others.

How would you describe a man who is addicted to pornography and spends his evenings immersed in all manner of sexual perversion? I imagine that you would call him a degenerate deviant who is quite sick. If you had a greater understanding, though, you might say that his past that drives him is what is disgusting, corrupt, and depraved. I am not excusing his behavior; God will judge that. But I would condone the argument that if you had his past, you might not be faring nearly as well as he is.

For if you knew that the man had been repeatedly sexually molested by his father at a very young age, you might agree that his past is a tragedy and that if he could have had another's past, he might be driven to church instead of to a porno house.

Our root problem is that the inner life's identity controls us. If we could destroy this identity of what we are at our worst and replace it with a new one, then daily events would not have power over us; we would have no need to become angry and rebellious, coping with our varied idols.

CHAPTER 7
The Loss of Self-life

Paul, in his letter to the Corinthians, describes the suffering that he is going through and concludes that "we do not lose heart, but though our outer man is decaying, yet our inner man is being renewed day by day" (II Corinthians 4:16). He brings out the fact that man possesses both an inner and outer life. It takes both of these lives to make up the unique person that is you.

How many different forms of outer life are there in the world today? We are all human; however, each of us makes a slightly different configuration. Therefore, there would presently be approximately five billion different forms of outer life.

How many different forms of inner life are there? If by some capability we could command the inner lives to step out of the people standing before us, all from different races and cultures, how many different types of inner life would we see? We would find that there are only two races of inner life, Adam-life or Christ-life, one of which would step out of each of the ten (Romans 5:14-18).

Being born in the likeness of Adam in our inner life causes us a number of problems, for Adam-life hates the commandments of God. In our minds we receive the commands and believe that they are good. All of us have experienced this conflict. We know what to do but are not able to follow through. I have yet to talk to an alcoholic or drug addict who did not concur with my observations of the negative effects of drugs on his physical body, his family, and his very emotional state. The problem was not in the area of understanding or information, but rather in the area of power.

Knowledge is not the problem; there is a power within that is greater than knowledge and willpower, and that is the Adam-life.

People attend conferences and seminars that explain the steps to be followed to have a good marriage and family life. It all sounds so good as they listen and busily take notes. The problem is implementation! The first day they may do fairly well, the next a little worse, and by the third day they have forgotten completely the principles learned.

Neither do the problems end with this Adam-life within that hates the commands of God. Picture outside of a person an unholy trinity, for just as there is a holy Trinity, there is an unholy one composed of sin, Satan, and the world. This unholy trinity possesses a certified copy of this person's history, which it has read very thoroughly. It waits until the ideal opportunity and throws him the perfect temptation. The inner life, which hates God's commands, cooperates fully to comply with the various aspects of the temptation, thus making the person a slave in the hopeless state of being powerless to say no and manifesting the condition of flesh. Next, the unholy trinity begins to work in the area of guilt; this is where the real damage is done. It will tell this person that his actions confirm the identity—what he feared might be true about him—that he received from the past. Within this process of temptation and slavery, the inner life is further denigrated.

This whole cycle and condition is described by one word: *flesh*. The flesh is the condition wherein a man is controlled by something other than God, in the world without hope, close to being destroyed, and enslaved by chains that no man can break. It may be to something obvious that one is enslaved, such as pornography or drugs; but it can also be to something such as television, eating, exercising, or something in the hidden areas of the heart, such as slander, gossip, bitterness, and contention. It does not matter; all of us are born with Adam-life and therefore are enslaved to something.

At some point in everyone's life this condition of slavery, no matter what form it has taken, is recognized. People also come to realize that their identity is not at all what they would like it to be. One word enters their minds: *change*! Mankind wants to change. This is evidenced by simply taking a trip to the local bookstore; in it are row after row of books written on the topic of change, anything from crystals and chants to exercise and horoscopes. All such books are a testimony to man's inability to change.

As we have noted, the unholy trinity works through the Adam-life to make one a slave to sin. Therefore, sin is not the problem, but rather the Adam-life that works with the unholy trinity. We have also indicated that it is the developed identity of the Adam-life that so often controls a person. Therefore, when we are discussing what needs to change, all evidence points to the Adam-life.

How can we get to the Adam-life to change it? It is the inner life! If I took a man into surgery and told the doctors to operate on his inner life, where would they begin to cut? What methods are tried to change this inner life that is so vexing? Counseling? Reading the Bible? Vowing never to commit a particular sin again? Attending seminars that give lists of what to do? Many are ready to admit that nothing has worked in the attempt to change. In fact, things may have even gotten much worse. Why? It is because man cannot change the manifestation of the flesh by working harder in the power of the flesh. Flesh will not improve flesh!

Since flesh is the condition of being controlled by something other than God, a Christian who is drawing upon his own resources and walking in unbelief and self-centeredness will often manifest the same characteristics that an unbeliever does. His condition is also entitled walking in the flesh. The flesh will not improve but only strengthen itself; the Bible is quite clear on this point. "That which is born of the flesh is flesh . . ." (John 3:6); " . . . the flesh profits nothing . . ." (John 6:63); "because by the works of the Law no flesh will be justified in His sight . . ." (Romans 3:20); ". . . the flesh is hostile toward God . . . those who are in the flesh cannot please God" (Romans 8:7, 8). The more one works to be transformed in the power of the flesh, the worse things will get. For example, a man drinking because he is in control of his own life (living independently of God, whether a believer or unbeliever) is in the flesh. If this same man takes charge and stops drinking, he is still in the flesh. That is why alcoholism is progressive for the man who lives in the flesh, even while he is sober.

Imagine, if you will, that my arm has in it a minor twitch which I find quite annoying. In fact, often when I am lecturing, my arm without warning will swing up and hit my eye! I devise a plan whereby I can overcome the twitch; I will lift weights until my arm becomes so strong that when it begins to jerk, I will hold it in place through my great strength. Soon after my arm reaches the desired proportions, my wife finds me lying on the floor, out cold with a black eye. When I come to and she asks what happened, I reply, "I twitched." You see, what used to annoy me has now been strengthened to the point that it might kill me.

So it is with the flesh; we cannot improve our condition in its power. If we cannot change our inner life and have learned that lesson all too well, then what are we to do? The answer is really quite ingenious: We simply exchange it! Our Adam-life is not to be patched up, as many religions and psychology teach, but put to death and exchanged for a new life!

The Exchanged Life

That is right, that vexing inner life—that Adam-life, its alliance with the unholy trinity, and its controlling identity—cannot be changed. It has been exchanged. This rests not one bit on the efforts or knowledge of man, but rather on the undertaking and wisdom of God.

As we have already stated, the inner and outer lives together make up "you." If we take out your inner life and replace it with another, you are no longer "you." You may look the same to everyone, but you are not, for the outer *and* inner lives compose what is uniquely "you." Exchanging the inner life makes you something quite different than you were before.

This is exactly what happens when a person is born again; he receives a new life and actually becomes a new person. In fact, he is no longer the same type of human, possessing Adam-life, but is a child of God, acquiring the life of Christ. That Adam-life that hates God's commands and is inadequate, insecure, worthless, and unacceptable is exchanged for Christ's life, acceptable, righteous, holy, and triumphant over the unholy trinity. "I have been crucified with Christ, and it is no longer I who live, but Christ lives in me; and the life which I now live in the flesh I live by faith in the Son of God, who loved me, and delivered Himself up for me" (Galatians 2:20).

The old you, consisting of the same outer body but with the Adam-life inside, has been put to death, giving way to the new you with Christ's life dwelling within. "Therefore if any man is in Christ, he is a new creature; the old things passed away; behold, new things have come" (II Corinthians 5:17). You are a new creation, something different! At this point we are not concerned about experience but truth! What God says, we believe. We are free from the condition of flesh because of our co-crucifixion with Christ.

Read Romans 6 and discover the spiritual realities of our baptism into Christ; we are set free from the power of sin and thus enter into true salvation. As discussed previously, the word *salvation* in Scripture refers to being delivered in the present. The spiritual significance of baptism is that we can participate in His death and be freed from the life that is in bondage to sin. Some will say that this is teaching baptismal regeneration (which I categorically deny) and that unless someone is baptized he will not go to heaven. Not so! What allows one to participate in heaven is the fact that he has been born again through faith, and that same faith in the blood of Jesus has taken away the penalty of sin. However, baptism is a spiritual reality in which we are set free from the bondage, not penalty, of sin. Baptism is not a work we do that saves us, but a participation in the work that He has done which delivers us, a spiritual reality. Without question thousands of baptized believers are walking around in defeat; it is quite obvious that baptism had no spiritual impact on their lives, but how could it? Baptism must be accompanied by faith, and faith cannot be exercised unless we have been taught what the spiritual realities are. Baptism is a spiritual reality wherein we can experience freedom from the power of sin and the old nature. "Or do you not know that all of us who have been baptized into Christ Jesus have been baptized into His death?" (Romans 6:3)

New Creation

The spiritual reality of participating in His death is great, for through it we have actually become something new, with the Adam-life put away. Not only did Christ die on that day but we with Him.

You may not know it, feel it, or experience it, but the day you came to Christ your old nature was removed and replaced with Christ's life. What is the significance of this?

In Galatians 2:20 (NIV) Paul says, "I have been crucified with Christ, and I no longer live." Of which "I" is Paul speaking, the new or the old me? Of course, the old. He then says, "the life which I now live"; he is now referring to the "new me." You see, Paul makes it quite clear that something died, and yet he is more alive than he has ever been. The advantage of our death with Christ is great, for the Adam-life that was so self-centered, insane, and controlled was put to death. When the Holy Spirit reveals this truth, the release is tremendous.

For instance, the man who had been controlled all his life by the past event of being molested realized that his old self had been put to death. Not only could he no longer be controlled by the past, but he saw that God had even given him a new self that had never been molested. He had grasped the truth that what had happened to his old man had not happened to his new man.

Freedom From Guilt

It is also true that what the "old me" did, the "new me" has never done. Many Christians are controlled by the guilt of past failures, sins, and events. Not only does the enemy not allow them to forget their sins, but often their own families and other Christians continue to remind them. I have often thought that a Christian whose family continued to remind him of past sins should buy a grave lot and erect a tombstone bearing the date on which he was born again. Then, when charged, he could drive the accusers to the gravesite and tell them to complain to the person buried there, but not to the new him!

The proof that your life has been exchanged and that the "old you" is dead is that whenever you remember or are reminded of the activities of the old you, it makes you somewhat sick! Why? Because the "new you" does not align itself with such things.

> Do not be deceived; neither fornicators, nor idolaters, nor adulterers, nor effeminate, nor homosexuals, nor thieves, nor the covetous, nor drunkards, nor revilers, nor swindlers, shall inherit the kingdom of God. And such were some of you; but you were washed, but you were sanctified, but you were justified in the name of the Lord Jesus Christ, and in the Spirit of our God.
>
> —I Corinthians 6:9-11

It is true that what described the "old you" by way of identity would not at all describe the "new you." As Watchman Nee so aptly points out in *The Normal Christian Life*, when we receive Christ's life, everything that was true about His life becomes true of our life. Just as what was true of Adam (his disobedience) became true of us, in a like manner, now that we have Christ's life all that is true of Him is true of us. What is true about Christ's life? It is righteous, it is victorious over the unholy trinity, it is not of this world, and it has overcome all obstacles, just to mention a few. Therefore, all of these things must also be true of the "new you."

You Are Acceptable

Imagine that when I arrive home one night, the neighbor kids playing in the yard with my children have been perfect angels. They have not thrown rocks, fought, or used bad language. Yet suppose that my children did all of these things. At suppertime, who will be invited in to eat, the neighbor children or my children? Mine, of course! But the neighbor children acted better, so why are they not invited in? For the simple reason that they have the wrong last name and are not my children.

One day there will be a great feast in heaven, and those who attend will not do so on the basis of their works, but on the basis of their birth. They must have the appropriate last name, "Children of the Most High God." Our co-crucifixion, burial, and new life (Christ's life) afford us that privilege.

We must say it again: All that is true about Christ's life is true of the "new you." Do you see the importance of this? Each inner life (Adam-life) has taken its own peculiar form because of the events, temptations, and the sins of the past. One has become a slanderer, one a homosexual, another an alcoholic, one a murderer, another a bitter loner, and the list goes on. But each one has the opportunity of exchanging what he has become for what Christ has always been.

One day I was eating in a restaurant and sharing the Lord with a friend. The man behind me overheard the conversation, and when I was leaving, he identified himself as a Christian and a recovering alcoholic. I stuck out my hand immediately and responded, "Nice to meet you. I'm Mike, a child of God." Then I asked him, "Which would you rather be, a recovering alcoholic or a child of God?" He returned to the office with me and we shared the exchanged-life truths. Again, there are two ways to be controlled by alcohol: One is needing it and the other is having to stay away from it. Either way, one's identity remains the same, an alcoholic.

Jesus did not come, however, so we could remain the same and merely be sinners who do not sin. He took away the life in us that desires sin and replaced it with a heavenly one: His very life. We possess a new identity; now we are saints, not sinners. Satan's definition of a hypocrite and God's are totally different. Satan tells us when we try to act holy we are hypocrites, because we are really wicked, vile sinners. On the other hand, God tells us we are hypocrites when we sin, because we are really holy saints! Even to the church in Corinth, with all her problems and sins, Paul addressed his letter to saints. Remember, we are not saints because of works, but by birth.

Working to Reveal vs. Working to Become

One thing that we have surely learned by this point is

that behavior cannot change what we are. We are what we are by birth, and to change we must be born again. Again, Christian growth is simply accepting what we have always been from the first day we accepted Christ. The word *grow* teaches this very thing, as it means to expand what already exists. "And the child continued to grow . . ." (Luke 1:80); "Consider the lilies, how they grow . . ." (Luke 12:27); "the word of the Lord continued to grow . . ." (Acts 12:24); ". . . grow up in all aspects into Him . . ." (Ephesians 4:15); ". . . grow in respect to salvation" (I Peter 2:2); and, "but grow in the grace and knowledge . . ." (II Peter 3:18). The same Greek word for "grow" is used in each of the preceding verses. We are not called to change into something but rather to expand what we already are. We are what we are by birth, and either we are growing in bondage to Adam's life or growing in the freedom of Christ's life.

One New Year's Eve I was spending my time on the streets of a major city witnessing to the people who passed by. I was invited into a female impersonators' bar by some of the occupants. I obliged, and upon entering the bar began to share the Gospel. I noticed a very large man sitting in the corner wearing a dress. I made my way over to him and began to share Christ with him. As I did, he began to cry and tell how miserable his life was and how he had to sneak out so his wife would not find out about his habits. In the end he got on his knees and asked Christ to enter his life. As I left that evening, I gave him a command, "Go home and put on men's clothes." Did I give him the command to change or to reveal what he really was? To reveal what he was! The man was quite confused about what he was, but I was not. He looked like a large man in a dress to me. As long as he was confused about what he was, he had difficulty being a man and difficulty being a woman.

If you are born again, your old Adam-life has been put to death and replaced with Christ's very life. Does the New Testament give you commands to change or to reveal what you are? To reveal, of course. You are commanded to be holy because you *are* holy! Why? Christ's life in you is holy. In all of Paul's letters, he spends the first half telling believers who they are before he begins to tell them what to do. If we know who we are, then the doing is natural.

Do you work to get God's acceptance or work because you are accepted? Do you read your Bible and pray to get God near to you or because He is near to you? Are you working to be holy, or working because you are? As you can see, it is the difference between life and death in the Christian experience.

Satan has gone to great lengths to blind Christians to the complete work of Christ. Many see Him only as the sacrifice for their sins; they do not realize that in receiving His very life and the crucifixion of the old self we can be as free from sin as Christ is. This is true salvation: to be free from the old identity and unholy trinity. Most Christians look as ridiculous as the big man in a dress, trying first men's clothes and then women's, but not knowing which he is to wear. Just so, the carnal believer walks after the flesh and then makes attempts to walk after the Spirit, never really knowing which fits best. Someone should stop the poor unbelieving believer and clear up his confusion by telling him, "You are born of God" (see John 3:3-7); "You are a child of God" (see I John 3:1, 2); "You are not of this world" (see John 17:16); "You are a new creation" (see II Corinthians 5:17); "You are His workmanship" (see Ephesians 2:10): "You are righteous" (see II Corinthians

6:14, 15); "You are a chosen race, a royal priesthood, a holy nation . . ." (I Peter 2:9).

Throw away those old garments of sin, failure, and defeat, and put on Christ. Let me remind you one more time about the wolf boy. He had lived so long as a wolf that when he was captured and attempts were made to persuade him that he was in fact a boy, even a mirror with his own image could not compel him to believe it. The baggage and residue of being a wolf was so strong in his mind, will, and emotions that he could not believe the truth. It took years to make his lying emotions agree with reality. Right now your emotions may agree with Satan's lie that you are just a sinner trying to please God—and a failure at that—but please remember what the mirror (the Bible) is telling you: You are a new creation, and what is true of Christ is true of you. Just as this boy's new parents did not give up on him until he came to the awareness that he was human, so can you trust your Father in heaven not to give up on you until you admit you are His child in every way.

Now we must answer the question that is so often raised. If my old self (old nature, Adam-life) has been put to death and I have received a new life, Christ's life, with everything that is true about Him being true about me, why do I still feel the same?

Continued Conflict?

One of the problems associated with unbelief is its tendency to protect God. By that I mean if God has spoken on a particular subject, and yet we have not been able to experience it, we cannot admit that the fault lies within us, but neither can we let the blame lie with God. We must, therefore, whitewash what God has spoken and give it an alternate meaning, thus protecting God and at the same time freeing ourselves from the accusation that we might be failing. This is especially true when it comes to the supernatural aspects of our relationship with God.

We believe with Paul, "I have been crucified with Christ; and it is no longer I who live, but Christ lives in me" (Galatians 2:20); and, "knowing this, that our old self was crucified with Him"; and again, "we have died with Christ . . ." (Romans 6:6, 8). Yet we have to admit that we still sometimes find ourselves in the same sins, behaviors, and feelings that we had before we were crucified with Christ and born again. Why?

Some have suggested that the reason is that the Adam-life or old nature never really died. He merely moved over, Christ's life moved in next to him, and the Christian possesses two natures that battle against one another.

The illustration is often used of the man who possessed two dogs, one black and the other white. When asked which dog was the strongest, the man replied, "The one I feed, of course." The point is then made that now that Christ dwells in us, we have the option to feed His life and walk by the Spirit, or feed the old nature or Adam-life and walk in the flesh. The explanation is an attempt to answer a legitimate question, which is, "If my old self is dead, why do I still feel it?" However, the concept of having two opposing forces or natures dwelling within us is—besides being contradictory to Scripture—hardly novel. We find that notion in most world religions, many of which predate Christianity, and most notable of which is Taoism, which has a similar teaching concerning the yin and yang. Its symbol of good and evil forces' warring against one another is a circle half filled with white and half filled with black. If we were to draw a trunk on this symbol, what we would have is the tree of the knowledge of good and evil! Adam ate from that tree, and men continue to eat from it; therefore, it is not surprising to find elements—that to the mind make sense—of this in religion.

Many portray Christianity as also coming from that tree, seeing God as good and Satan as evil, with the whole religion centering around the warring of these two opposing forces. The teaching that follows is quite simple: This is good, this is evil; do good, not evil! However, Christianity does not originate in the tree from which all other religions do; it springs from the other tree that was in the Garden, the tree of Life, rooted in the person of the Lord Jesus and based on something much deeper than a mere struggle between good and evil.

In John 15, Jesus uses the illustration of the vine and the branch. It is quite clear from nature that once a branch has been grafted on, its old life is completely replaced by new life from the vine. There is no warring between old and new lives. Even though the branch might remember what it felt like to be cut off and dead, it now receives a new and different life from only one source.

The Unrenewed Mind

We will reject the argument that the Christian has two natures and look to Scripture for a different explanation. Let us return to our illustration of the inner and outer lives, with the "old you" consisting of your present outer life and the Adam-life dwelling within. The unholy trinity (sin, Satan, world) devises a temptation tailor-made for the Adam-life, which would concur with it and make you a slave to sin. Every sin that was committed, idol trusted, and identity message received had to register in your mind, will, and emotions (your soul); and, therefore, the complete history of your old nature is stored there. When the old man is put to death and replaced by Christ's life and Spirit, you are one with Him and He with you (John 17:21). "Moreover, I will give you a new heart and put a new spirit within you; and I will remove the heart of stone from your flesh and give you a heart of flesh. And I will put my Spirit within you and cause you to walk in My statutes, and you will be careful to observe My ordinances" (Ezekiel 36:26, 27). You receive a new spirit, but your old soul containing the old information remains.

At some point in your life you probably touched something hot and were burned. That event is registered in your mind, and even though the pain suffered from it has long since passed, the remembrance of it remains. I would imagine that if you lived to be 150 years old you would still remember that hot things burn. In the same way, the events, emotions, choices, sins, and idols of the old nature still remain in you.

Many of us have had the experience of having someone close to us die. Long after the loved one's death, we may come upon some of his personal belongings, which will stir up our emotions. Even though he is no longer with us, much baggage from his life with us remains for years. I even heard of one woman who kept her baby's room exactly as it had been on the day of her child's death over fifteen years earlier. She enjoyed going into the room and stirring up old feelings. Again, the baby is gone but the baggage remains.

The baggage that we accumulated by living with the old nature for years is still stored in the mind, will, and emotions. Is it any wonder that we are commanded in Romans 12:2 to renew our minds? Understanding the residue or baggage that was left by the Adam-life will help us to understand how a Christian can walk with the Lord, in the Spirit, for days, weeks, and even years, and in an instant find himself attracted to the old sins, idols, and feelings of the past.

I would like you to imagine Christ's life dwelling in you, about where your heart is, and just above that life a door that opens and closes; we will call it "the abiding door." What opens the abiding door is humility, and what closes it is pride.

If there could be one word that describes God, it would be *love*, but the one word that might best describe Jesus is *humility*. Humility is not saying, "I am nothing"; rather, the humble man says, "I have nothing." Jesus emptied Himself, taking the form of a man; He possessed nothing, yet He was the Son of God. In divine obedience, He received moment by moment what He needed from the Father. Jesus did not walk on water because He could, but because God told Him to. He could have said wonderful things when the woman who was caught in adultery was brought to Him, but He drew on the ground in readiness for what God would have Him say. In fact, the New Testament does not record any original saying of Jesus, for He Himself said He only spoke what the Father told Him to. He was Divine Humility.

That same spirit of humility allows us to recognize that we have nothing and that our very existence must be supported by the Father moment by moment. When we live in that recognition, the imaginary door above Christ's life swings open wide, allowing His life to flow. As it does,

He does some housecleaning, as it were, removing the baggage of the old nature and at the same time expressing through us new life. If in pride we decide that we possess resources to better deal with daily life than He, at that moment the door closes to His life, and the unholy trinity seizes the opportunity to lure us with a temptation arising from something in our past. Since we have shut the door to Christ, we open up the baggage from the old nature that remains in the mind, will, and emotions, looking for something that will allow us to cope with the situation.

In the first ten years of a certain couple's marriage, the woman had dominated and controlled her husband, making him miserable. Then she came to Christ and for the next year allowed her husband to be head of the house. The husband thought the transformation was wonderful. However, without warning the woman once again began to dominate and control her husband, who at this point was completely confused, believing he lived with a schizophrenic. But I can assure you he was not as confused as she was.

The dynamics of what had happened involved the wife's growing up watching her mother relate to men by controlling and dominating. When she married, the enemy naturally tempted her to do the same with her husband. When she came to Christ, the old nature that had made her act that way was removed, and for one year she trusted the Lord moment by moment for all things, thus opening the abiding door. Her husband felt he was living with an angel! But when the pressure was turned on and she was afraid that her husband would not respond as he should, she began to think, *What shall I do?* Thoughts of independence arose and closed the door. The enemy moved in to tempt her to dominate and control, two idols left in the old baggage that had worked for her in the past. As we noted, God will not allow the old idols of a new creation to work, which caused her anxiety and depression.

The problem, I am sure both she and her husband would say, is that she is once again domineering. However, before she was born again her problem was not dominating and controlling but the Adam-life that made her a slave to that behavior. We could have worked on domination and control for years and never resolved it, for it had to find its demise in co-crucifixion. As she found herself once again acting in this manner, deception would lead her to try to change the behavior, when the trouble is that she has shut the abiding door through pride and unbelief.

This explains why we can often see the same behavior in an unbeliever that we do in an unbelieving believer. We may see a man getting drunk both before he is a Christian and after he has been born again; however, we must be careful not to judge this man as not really being a Christian, for he may only have the door to Christ's life closed. The door can open and close as fast as a thought. Many believe that it can close as fast as a wicked thought, but few know that it also will open just as fast with a repentant prayer. You may say, "This does not sound like abundant life to have to continually busy myself with keeping that door open!" or "So what if the old nature is gone? The baggage makes me act the same and live just as miserably!" These concerns will be addressed more fully in the next chapter.

Satan's Fear Of An Open Door

If you choose to believe and walk in your co-crucifixion with Christ, life will often get worse before it gets better, with dangers increasing. For you become a threat to the enemy! Before, when you functioned only in natural talent, ability, and intellect, and your old identity tried so hard to change yourself and others, you were no menace to him; on the contrary, you were one of Satan's great assets. But as Christ lives His life through you, you are dangerous! You are able to walk as Christ walked, crushing the head of the devil, who must mount an attack to persuade you that your experience, not faith in what God says, must be your measure of truth. I like to warn people I disciple that as soon as they leave, Satan will tell them that I attempted to brainwash them and that reality consists of their experiences of being failures, being worthless, and feeling rejected by God because their behavior is not good enough. The enemy has yet to disappoint me in this matter. The opposite, however, is true: The enemy is the one who wishes to brainwash them, because brainwashing is convincing someone that a lie is the truth.

Satan's plan is very simple; he must get you out of the light! Why? "For with Thee is the fountain of life; in Thy light we see light" (Psalm 36:9). I have personally found that Jesus makes life make sense, and once I find myself out of His light, life has no center or meaning. Therefore, the enemy wants to draw us out of Christ's light into his darkness. Then, ever so subtly and unbeknownst to us, the door closes. Being in darkness, our eyes slowly adjust and it becomes normal for us. With the passing of time we forget how wonderful it was to dwell in the light, so we begin to look for a small candle (a person, an idol, a job, some pursuit of happiness) that when lit will make the present darkness tolerable. We are, in a word, defeated!

The enemy has myriad tricks to take us into darkness.

Usually he will begin to tempt us with the same kind of situations and events that gave us our negative identities from the past. He will try to push our buttons, so to speak, to drive us back to a carnal existence.

Imagine that you have worked in the same building for the last twenty years, and every day you have gone to the soda-pop machine, put in the money, pushed a button, and gotten your drink. Then one day you put in the money and push the button, but no soda pop comes out! Will you walk away or get frustrated and begin to hit the button frantically, wondering where the soda is?

There are certain buttons the enemy has pushed for years to make you ineffective; once you are living out of Christ's life, he will not simply go away! On the contrary, he will push buttons all the more frantically to get the responses of the past. When you see this happening, do take heart, for you have truly found the answer; if you had not, the enemy would not be attacking you.

It is the enemy who would continually stir the emotions, and the more we walk in the Lord, the more our emotions are calmed. When Satan sees this, he will work all the harder to arouse them.

Have you ever watched a heart monitor? As the heart beats there are peaks and lows on the screen, but when the heart dies there is a steady line. The doctors will then massage and even pound on the heart in hopes of bringing back the peaks and lows. To the uninformed observer, the treatment can look very harsh.

Instead of a heart monitor, think of an emotional monitor, which the enemy loves to see have peaks and lows. When we begin to walk in the will of God, there will be a more steady line, for the emotions begin to respond to what is occurring in the spirit rather than in the body or circumstances. The enemy will try everything at his disposal to emotionally beat a believer, in hopes of seeing the lows and peaks return. Be watchful; it may happen when we are on vacation and out of the daily fellowship we normally have with our Savior. It may occur during times of stress, when our relationships with others are strained, or when we are under such financial pressure that we seek the so-called security the world offers. It may be the result of a person whose situation or action draws our eyes off the Lord, such as a child in trouble, the illness of a parent, or the rebellion of a mate. On a trip home to visit mother and father--the very people who most likely gave us many of the old identity messages, and with whom we had likely experienced a status quo relationship for years as unregenerate persons--all the old feelings and responses can be stirred up once more. Even our work for the Lord can become so important that we neglect Him. It can especially take place in times of loneliness and failure. The list is endless, but the result is the same: We close the door to His life, and in so doing, we begin to live much as we did before we were born again.

Not only will the enemy use circumstances and people, but he will attack with a new level of temptations that the unregenerate world rarely experiences. These are the enemy's Grade-A temptations, well-planned, exactly timed, with every detail considered. These temptations can take years to fully develop, as minor deceptions that may be as much as 99 percent truth are moved into place over time.

In India I once watched a man as he blasted away huge boulders three times the size of an automobile. I asked what he would do with such large rocks and was told he would make small gravel by hand to be used on roads. He would sit day after day, chiseling away at the rock, and as the boulders became smaller, the pile of gravel would grow. It was hard to believe that one man could do this, but obviously he had a plan, and the element of time saw him through to the end.

So it is with the deep deceptions of the enemy. If we knew his plan for destruction ahead of time, we would think it impossible. However, if we knew his timetable and the effort that would be placed into the deception day by day, we would be filled with fear. Is it any wonder we are called to be alert, stand fast, take heed, and not be ignorant of the enemy?

These deep deceptions are likened to seeds. When a seed is first planted, who would imagine that a mighty oak could one day stand in its place? For when the seed is underground, we are unaware of its existence, though it is growing every day. It is so often true of seeds that by the time their presence is revealed, it is too late to do anything about them. The spiritual man must be aware of temptations that are not calculated to bring immediate defeat, but downfall years away.

The Way Out of a Closed Door

Let us assume we are living in defeat. What happens next? "Greater is He who is in you than he who is in the world." God is much greater than the enemy; this we must not forget! By His own action He will reveal our condition, for God alone can break through the darkness in which Satan has the carnal Christian living. When it happens, it is as if you are sitting in your living room in the middle of the night, with the blinds pulled shut and all the lights out, when lightning strikes and for an instant every object in every corner is visible. With the light of the Holy Spirit, the deceptions of the enemy can be seen clearly. This no man can do; it must be the work of the Holy Spirit. "Well then, *God* has granted to the Gentiles also the repentance that leads to life" (Acts 11:18, emphasis mine), and, "with gentleness correcting those who are in opposition, if perhaps God may grant them repentance leading to the knowledge of the truth" (II Timothy 2:25). This God will do, contrary to all of the enemy's efforts, in His own timing. When our eyes are opened, many times we are undone. We cannot believe it! How did we allow this sin to creep into our lives? What are we to do? What can be done?

When any of us realize through this enlightenment the error of our way, the enemy steps up the attack for fear that all of his long efforts and deep deceptions might be for naught. He begins to whisper in a voice that is calculated to be confused with conscience, "It has been too long; you have fallen too far and do not have the strength to return." "You will only be a phony if you try." "You are a fake." "God has cut you off because of the length and depth of your sin." "You had your chance." "You are not saved." "You cannot do any better." It is all said in hopes that we will not return to God and learn His true character.

This book is for the defeated, as mentioned in the preface. If there is one thing I pray you would receive out of the book, it is this, so please take it to heart: *The true depth of a person's faith is revealed in his ability to accept forgiveness in the midst of his deepest defeat.* It is easy to believe that your righteousness is based in Christ when you have not done anything wrong, but you may have a confidence that is not based on Christ's work but on your own. When you have done nothing wrong, perhaps the thought of death does not frighten you because you are carrying with you a nice little bag of good works with which you think the Lord will be pleased. However, failure reveals where you have really put your trust; if in its midst you shrink back in fear, you prove that your righteousness was based on what you could do and not on what He has done. Many in the midst of failure refuse forgiveness, continuing a self-inflicted punishment until they believe they have paid the price. Some are so unbelieving that they even begin to make up excuses for why God should not forgive them.

The New Testament writers are not surprised by the fact that saints do sin, and their solution is simple: repentance and pressing on. If we were to apply Jesus' standard of what sin is to leaders ("as a man thinks in his heart") and remove any found sinning accordingly, I question whether we would have anyone at all to lead. We forget that ministry is a gift from God that is exercised as the door to His life in us is opened. Ministry does not come from a man's own righteousness. If a leader sins, he must follow the New Testament prescription for sin and go on:

> Submit therefore to God. Resist the devil and he will flee from you. Draw near to God and He will draw near to you. Cleanse your hands, you sinners, and purify your hearts, you double-minded. Be miserable and mourn and weep; let your laughter be turned into mourning, and your joy to gloom. Humble yourselves in the presence of the Lord, and He will exalt you.
>
> —James 4:7-10

Yes, when you see your sin and deception you will be undone, and this will cause mourning, but God will exalt you. The Bible does not say that God will restore you merely to a position somewhat lower than you had before; it says that He will exalt you!

If you have ever once experienced freedom from your failure, you can experience it once again, for it is moment by moment. If as a believer you have shut the door, repent, accept His forgiveness in spite of how you feel, and press on. Shortening the time span that you allow yourself to wallow after defeat will conversely give an increased time of victory.

The Three Selves

As they begin to study the topic of co-crucifixion, many become confused as to what exactly has been crucified with Christ. Not only do the best-known authors on the topic use different terms when describing what died and what must be denied, but so do the variety of Bible translations available. I will attempt to clear this up a little by describing the three different selves that appear in Scripture.

The unique self is that part of a person that was made in the womb by God (Psalm 139). As God is not in the cookie-cutting business, He makes us as individuals; and although we all have the same purpose in life, which is to fellowship with Him, we will all, as unique creations, express that fellowship in different ways. I will, therefore, define *unique self* as the creation of God that is distinctive to each person; that would include one's God-given talents, abilities, intellect, personality, and temperament.

In some ways you can think of the unique self as a tool that can do nothing on its own, but derives its value from how it is used and by whom. For example, a hammer is a hammer. What will distinguish the hammer is who uses it and what is accomplished by it. It could be used by a madman to kill someone or by a generous man to build a widow a home. The same is true of the unique self. The unique self cannot be changed, but its source and purpose can be exchanged.

Self #1, then, is the unique self under the control of Adam-life; this self belongs to the unbeliever, or unregenerate man, producing a condition called flesh. A man may possess the God-given ability to start businesses by motivating and persuading others to follow, as well as the natural talent necessary. However, with the old nature in control, the talent and ability that were created to express God instead reveal a condition of flesh, and the man may open a chain of adult bookstores. He has distorted God's gift of unique self and used it for sin, pleasure, and his own purposes.

God's command concerning this Self #1 is that it be crucified (Galatians 2:20), although what it is that dies is the source of the unique self, what is driving it, but not the actual unique self. Self #1 has a course set in one direction, and it follows every signpost leading it that way. Its destination is hell.

The second of the three selves (Self #2) is the unique self under the control of the baggage and residue of the dead and removed Adam-life and the unholy trinity. This person is a born-again believer in a carnal condition. He might use all of the God-given abilities to start a ministry or business that will be for his own glory, financial security, and use. This person is assured of going to heaven but will continue to experience hell on earth! The command regarding this self is to deny it daily (Luke 9:23) by the power of the cross.

Self #3 is very important, being the unique self under the control of Christ's life within. The man in this state enters into the fullness of his being. All of his God-given talents, abilities, intellect, personality, and temperament function properly as they should, and he manifests a condition called walking in the Spirit. Whatever work the man does, Christ does through him, and he is a blessing to all. When Christ controls the unique self, the boundary between spiritual work and secular work disappears, for all labor is spiritual and of Christ. It does not bother Self #3 to perform what some consider to be menial tasks, just so Christ is the source. God's perspective of a valuable work is quite different from man's view. How many of us think of giving a small physical need to another as highly commendable? "And whoever in the name of a disciple gives to one of these little ones even a cup of cold water to drink, truly I say to you he shall not lose his reward" (Matthew 10:42).

I was once asked, "What would you do for the Lord if you could do anything?"

My response was, "If I could do anything at all for the Lord, I would go farm with my grandfather." Plowing and watching the seagulls follow behind eating the grubs that the loving Father has provided for them, satisfying my desire to spend time with a grandparent who gives me constant acceptance; yes, if I could do anything for the Lord, I would farm with my grandfather! Once the line between secular and spiritual disappears, the pressure to do something great for the Lord fades, for then even the simplest of tasks accomplished with Christ's life in control are great works in the eyes of the Father.

The commandment concerning Self #3 is that we are to love it. ". . . You shall love your neighbor as yourself" (Matthew 19:19).

You can see that it is somewhat confusing when we read that we are to have self crucified, to deny self, and at the same time we are to love ourselves. The above distinction should help clear up the confusion. We have spoken much of the death of Self #1, and particularly in the next chapter we will examine the denial of Self #2. I would like to briefly mention the need for love of the unique self as it submits to the Spirit's rule, Self #3.

A Closer Look at the Unique Self

When I disciple those critical of others, I immediately ask the question, "What is it about yourself that you do not like?" It will often be that they are not as intelligent as their friends, or as attractive, or as talented. Therefore, since they do not love what they are, they must tear everyone else down, finding flaws to ease their own inferiority.

We are to love our neighbors as we love ourselves. If that is true then most neighbors are in for a lot of disappointment when it comes to being loved. Those who possess great talent or ability in a particular area tend to build inferiority in those who cannot function as well as they do. For example, most evangelists are, in their unique selves, very outgoing and forceful; that is what they are by creation, and if they were not evangelists, they could be car salesmen. They come to the church and tell one story after another about their boldness for the Lord, covertly condemning others who are not so forward as being ashamed of the Gospel. They do not understand that God makes every member of the body for a different use (the "some sow and some reap" principle); therefore, they continue to exult in their abilities, proclaiming loudly the message that they live the successful (success being to do what they do) Christian life naturally. Unfortunately, when someone with this particular unique self pastors a church, he will often develop approaches that center around his natural abilities and not those of the whole congregation. He then finds himself having to force people to participate, and the programs are usually short-lived. If he could understand the distinctiveness of the variety of true selves that the Lord has made, the man would be much more useful as a leader. For there are those whose unique selves simply cannot go door to door, arguing and cajoling. But they are very competent in following up on any who are interested in pursuing a relationship with Christ.

There is a great variety of unique selves in the body of Christ, from those who love following a plan to those who never make a schedule, from those who love working with people to those who would rather deal with things. All who are expressing the nature of their unique selves under the control of Christ's life are a great blessing.

It will be important to discern between the three selves, the one that is crucified, the one to deny, and the one that is to be loved. The reason that I have spent considerable time explaining the baggage, residue, and old identity is so Self #2 can readily be recognized and denied. Otherwise, one could try to deny the unique self, the one God made, which is quite uncomfortable and unproductive to do.

Do you love yourself? You should! It may take some time to become pleased in what God has made you to be, but once you do, you will stop comparing yourself with others and begin to appreciate the rest of the body of Christ.

I once discipled a man who was a millionaire and asked him how he became one. He said it was quite simple; he subcontracted his weaknesses. That is, he did not surround himself with people who were exactly like him, but with those much different in their thinking and attitudes. It prompted a lot of disagreeing, but he kept going to the bank with more and more money. Many want to avoid conflict and surround themselves with those who think exactly like them, but they are never very productive. The body of Christ is productive in its diversity, not by molding everyone into the same type of unique self.

I am, as one dear brother told me, easily had. That is true, because I like people so much I often allow them to use me. God has utilized that trait of my unique self several times, in that I never give up on anyone and often see the Lord turn someone from defeat to victory. On the other hand, recognizing this characteristic has caused me to turn to my brothers who do not have it to aid me in decision-making. I am very grateful that they are not like me.

In I Samuel 30, David and his men were involved in a supernatural victory. Those who had been too tired to go to the battle were instructed to remain and keep guard over the baggage. Upon returning from the battle, some "wicked men" did not want to share the spoil with those who chose to stay back rather than fight. David's response was a strong no, for those who protected the baggage were worthy of as much spoil as those who fought. David would not forget that the victory really belonged to God, and after all, what is the purpose of going out to war to gain more if there is the possibility of losing what is already possessed?

There are those of us God puts on the frontlines to participate in His supernatural working, which must never be viewed as our work, and those of us God has put in charge of the baggage (what is already possessed), who will receive the same reward. God shows no partiality, and the first will be last and the last first. God creates those with great talent, ability, and intellect—no one creates himself—and therefore, boasting must not be in the unique self but rather in God alone.

You see, talent, ability, and intellect are relative. Each unique self has its own purpose and usefulness. We have different gifts, workings, manifestations, bodies, and nationalities, but the same Spirit. Each of us is a different individual, and yet we are all one; together we experience wholeness. Paul encouraged those who are not content with the unique self (and therefore judge God, their Creator) to love what they are, and at the same time warned those who take pride in what God has made them to be.

You may ask, "What is my unique self, and how can I discern it?" Knowing your unique self is simple and does not take prolonged inward vision. Your unique self is determined by those things that you do naturally and are most comfortable doing (this is different from the behaviors such as withdrawal, avoidance, and erroneous fears that may develop through false identity messages). Are you always late getting home because you talk to the gas station attendant or to a neighbor? Your unique self is a people person, a sensory member. If you have all the nuts, bolts, and screws in their proper places in the garage, then your unique self has been created to enjoy detail and do a job right. Do you want a specific plan for the job to be done and what your part will be? This unique self is a team person who wants to see the project through; you are an internal member. Are you easily bored, anxious to get on to the next project? You are a muscle member.

Just remember, however God has made you, enjoy yourself, love yourself, and refuse to listen to those who would intimidate by boasting of their natural abilities. Whatever measure He has given you, enjoy it. If you are not as intellectual as another, that was God's decision, and if you complain, you make yourself out to be the Creator. "Who are you, O man, who answers back to God? The thing molded will not say to the molder, 'Why did you make me like this,' will it?" (Romans 9:20) Remember, too, that the gifts of the Spirit rarely follow our normal traits; they are not the same as natural abilities, which even an unbeliever possesses, but are supernatural.

CHAPTER 8
Living Moment by Moment

In the previous chapter we learned that even though your old self was crucified with Christ and is dead and buried, you still have a mind cluttered with his baggage; and whenever the door just above your heart is closed to Christ's life, the enemy tempts you to dabble again in the garbage resident in the mind, causing you to live a replica of the life you did before becoming a Christian. We thought, *Does this sound like abundant life? What could God's purpose in all of this be?* His purpose is actually quite ingenious. It is to make your life moment by moment full of joy, excitement, and authenticity! How?

If God desires to love you, how many days out of the year does He want to love you? Your answer, I am quite sure, is 365 days out of every year. How many hours of every day would He like to love you? Twenty-four hours out of every day. How many minutes out of every hour and seconds out of every minute does He wish to love you? God desires to love sixty minutes out of every hour and sixty seconds out of every minute—you are quite right! Now, how many moments out of every second does He long to love you? The answer is moment by moment.

Having established that, let us suppose that you gave your life to Christ on October 12, 1970, at 9:30 p.m. What do that date and time have to do with this present moment? Absolutely nothing! If God desires you moment by moment, then He was satisfied on October 12, 1970, at 9:30 p.m., but that has nothing to do with the desire of this present moment!

Suppose I tell my wife to come and sit next to me, hold my hand, and talk with me, and her response is, "We did that fifteen years ago!"

What would my reaction be? Probably, "So what? I do not care what we did fifteen years ago! I am talking about now!"

Relationships ever flow; what makes them wonderful is not so much what happened in the past, but what is happening in the present moment. It does not matter that you got along with your husband the first year of your marriage; what matters is how you are getting along now.

Often someone who has been in active ministry for years but is currently living in defeat will recount all his past glories: the wonderful things he has done and how he has been mightily used for the Lord. He will describe his extended periods of prayer, times when the Lord would speak to him, and all the wondrous things done by God. It is quite obvious that such a one believes these things that happened years ago will perpetually carry him into the future with the Lord. Not so!

God has the aspiration to be in fellowship with us moment by moment; He also has a plan to bring about His wishes. First of all, He must destroy the old self that dwells within and replace it with the life of His Son. If this is not done, then no fellowship with Him is even possible. The next thing that He does is to leave all the baggage and residue from the old man in the mind. When through unbelief a person closes the door to His life within and consequently cuts off fellowship, of necessity all the baggage, garbage, residue, lying emotions, false feelings, old idols, inaccurate identity, and every manifestation of the flesh arise. In fact, this one is now more miserable than when dwelling in the world. God will strive to build the believer's awareness of a desire to be free from those miseries 365 days a year, 24 hours a day, 60 minutes an hour, 60 seconds a minute, yes, moment by moment! It is then that God can do business! You see, God structures our lives in such a way as to keep us ever near His side.

In the wilderness, the people of Israel were to go out and gather the manna for the day's food supply. There were some who, perhaps from laziness and a preference to stay in bed, would collect enough manna to last for two days. But what happened to the manna on the second day? It became foul and wormy (Exodus 16). In John 6, Jesus makes it clear that He is the true bread that comes down out of heaven: "I am the bread of life; he who comes to Me shall not hunger" (vs. 35). Jesus, just like the bread that fed Israel in the wilderness, is to be consumed daily, and if one tries to keep what he has savored of the Lord one day for the next, it will prove to be useless. Jesus is to be partaken of each day!

People often tell me they simply do not understand their condition. They explain that a few years ago they came to the place of giving up on all their own resolve and methods to save themselves and did, in fact, find real victory. This I do not question; they did come to the end of themselves several years ago. The problem is that they have not come to the end of themselves in the moment in which they are talking to me. It must be firmly implanted in our minds that victory is for one moment at a time, and that in any given moment we are participating in eternal victory or eternal defeat.

Right now it is 11:15 p.m. I do not possess 11:10 or 11:20 p.m.; I only possess 11:15. I must conclude that I am a creature of the moment; all that matters is this instant. If at 11:15 p.m. I have the door to Christ's life open, then I have a perpetual life flowing through me that has already overcome every temptation that I will ever have. Thus, at that moment I, too, am eternally victorious and do not worry about 11:20 p.m., tomorrow, next week, next year, the children, the job, or destiny, for I am eternally victorious. However, if at 11:15 p.m. I have closed the door, then I worry about 11:20 and what will happen. Again I am in charge, even though I am a failure, a worthless person, full of anxiety and depression; naturally I am apprehensive about tomorrow, next week, next month, the children, my marriage, even standing before the Lord. I am languishing in eternal defeat. Therefore, the only thing that Satan must accomplish to defeat me is to steal the moment, which he does by reminding me about the past or nudging my fears about the future!

Once after I spoke at a conference, a woman came to me saying that she could not get her eyes off the mistake that she had made. She had left a pot of boiling water close enough to the stove that her daughter could pull it off onto herself. The girl had suffered severe disfiguring burns. The mother said that she would sit at home and continually replay the mishap in her mind, condemning herself and crying. She had become totally dysfunctional. I explained the enemy's plan to steal the moment from her. Although there was no question that the event of twelve months ago was a very real tragedy, the greater calamity was that not only had the accident ruined the family climate, it had also continued to impair every moment since for a full year. The ordeal was bad enough, but worse was the situation in which the daughter was being punished by not having a functioning mother now, in the present moment.

Many Christians have allowed an incident in the past to continue to steal abundant life from them in moments that stretch into days and then years. One who allows this to happen is dancing with the devil, whose plan is to steal not just one moment, but the whole life!

Many have relinquished the present moment through unforgiveness; though they took place several years ago, memorable encounters may have access into their minds at any instant, stealing peace and joy. In unforgiveness the enemy has at his disposal a powerful tool to take life. We are reminded that love never keeps a list of wrongs, and those who walk in unforgiveness are rebels in the Kingdom of God, where love is not optional.

Abundant spiritual life is experienced moment by moment. The carnal mind sees the progression from a life of defeat to the life of victory somewhat like a staircase. Each time he does good, he takes one step up the staircase, and each time he complies with evil, he regresses one step.

The Book of Galatians teaches that our options are to walk after the flesh or in the Spirit, and there is no staircase. At any given moment one is either in the flesh or in the Spirit, tapped into eternal defeat or eternal victory.

Remember that many believe that the door to Christ's life can close as fast as a thought, but they do not believe that it can also open as quickly. What opens the door is humility, saying that one has nothing or, "I cannot!" What closes the door is pride, which says, "I can." God has so structured things that victory will only be moment by moment as we abide in Him.

There are two principles that can be learned from understanding that God leaves those things that vex you in order to keep you near to Him. First, if God leaves the baggage and the residue of the old self in the mind to make you miserable when you are not abiding, and therefore to drive you to Him where you experience eternal victory and joy, then let me ask you a question. Is the baggage and residue Satan's stronghold to destroy you or God's stronghold to bless and give you abundant life? It is God's stronghold! The very thing that you have been begging God to take away, which you believed would allow you full and unhindered service and fellowship with the King, is the very assurance God has that you will continue to fellowship with and serve Him. Praise God, His ways are not man's ways!

Do you see why I told the Christian who was struggling with homosexuality that he would be continually blessed of God if the only time that he was free from homosexual craving was when he was abiding in Christ with the door fully open? For some reason that we need not know, the majority of Christians are satisfied to walk away from the Lord; God allows it but is not content until He calls them back to Himself. Anyone who wants to go from the room called "Carnal" to the suite titled "Spiritual" must take the only doorway, named "Trouble, Suffering, and Defeat." So it is with all who are called to return to Him; they must pass through that doorway!

Second, the Lord spends considerable time teaching us to recognize the baggage and residue when it surfaces. Those old things (depression, unbelief, desire to do drugs) are flashing red lights informing us that the door is closed. Here is a secret: The more baggage that one has, the more flashing red lights he has, and the more he will be aware of his need to abide. The more one is aware of his need to abide, the more he will open the door and have Christ's life living through him. The person with well-adjusted flesh, with great natural talent, ability, and intellect, will most often not see his need for the Lord so dramatically, and will be slower to open the door and manifest the power of the Lord, merely displaying his own fleshly capacity.

> Because the foolishness of God is wiser than men, and the weakness of God is stronger than men. For consider your calling, brethren, that there were not many wise according to the flesh, not many mighty, not many noble; but God has chosen the foolish things of the world to shame the wise, and God has chosen the weak things of the world to shame the things which are strong, and the base things of the world and the despised, God has chosen, the things that are not, that He might nullify the things that are, that no man should boast before God.
>
> — I Corinthians 1:25-29

Listen to what Paul says, ". . . there was given me a thorn in the flesh, a messenger of Satan to buffet me—to keep me from exalting myself! Concerning this I entreated the Lord three times that it might depart from me. And He said to me, 'My grace is sufficient for you, for power is perfected in weakness.' Most gladly, therefore, I will rather boast about my weaknesses, that the power of Christ may dwell in me" (II Corinthians 12:7-9). Paul was given a frailty that made him say, "I can't," which opened the door to Christ's life and caused His power to be released. The more weakness, the more power released; therefore, he would be proud of his limitations.

Do you realize, child of God, all that Satan had planned for your destruction, God has planned for your good? Satan may tailor-make a temptation to destroy you, but God will walk by and, with the snap of His fingers, change the newly designed funeral clothes into garments of celebration. God is never, I repeat, never outdone by Satan. Do not lament over your past failures, hurts, and identity; they have all been crucified, and their remembrance is but God's stronghold.

When Paul describes the fruit of the Spirit in Galatians 5, he is not describing what he would have the Galatians imitate, which would simply produce artificial fruit with no substance or value. Rather, Paul is describing what a believer manifests when the door to Christ's life is open. If you are naturally manifesting love, joy, peace, patience, kindness, and so on, you are enjoying life in the Spirit. However, if these are not present, you can be sure that the door has been closed.

Once a person has taken lessons in flying an airplane, he will always look at the gauges on which his life depends. They warn him if he is about to crash and keep him safe. Consider the baggage and residue of the mind as your gauges, and when they warn you that the door is closed, open it immediately so as not to miss one moment of His precious life. If you would experience abundant life, it must be embraced moment by moment!

The Moment-by-Moment Cross

In the last chapter we explained that the day we came to Christ and believed in Him we were crucified with Christ, received Christ's life, were born again, and thus became new creations. I would now like to make a closer examination of the wonder of our crucifixion with Christ.

I want to express appreciation for the great South African devotional writer of the late nineteenth and early twentieth centuries, Andrew Murray, who did considerable writing concerning the Christian's experience of abundant life. Several followed after him, building upon and teaching these principles, most notably Jessie Penn-Lewis, Watchman Nee, and more recently, F. J. Huegel. I am greatly indebted to the teachings of these saints, which the Holy Spirit used to make real for me the teachings of Romans 6.

I once discipled a woman who had been in bondage to alcoholism for several years. Once the Holy Spirit opened her eyes to the power of the cross, her co-crucifixion with Christ, and the fact that her alcoholic inner life had been put to death nearly two thousand years ago, she was radically transformed. She was no longer an alcoholic but a child of God, as free from alcohol as was the life within her (Christ's life). A few weeks later she returned to give me what she felt was some very exciting news: I was to speak at the alcohol treatment center that was not able to help her. She was persuaded that since God had set her free, all of the staff at the center would want to be trained to do the same thing that I had. I told her I would be happy to share with the staff. "But remember, I must share with them that victory comes only through death with Christ two thousand years ago."

She then acknowledged, "That really does sound crazy when you think about it. Maybe we should cancel the meeting."

Yes, indeed, it really does sound absurd when we think about it, but it is the foolishness of God that will be our power in salvation. We must be careful, then, not to strip this message of its foolishness, and in so doing deprive it of power. We ask the Holy Spirit to open the eyes of our hearts that He would make the foolishness of the cross not understandable teaching but revelation, for with revelation comes faith and power to experience what is taught.

Why is a sinner a sinner? Is it because he sins or because he is born a sinner and is therefore driven to sin? Watchman Nee uses an appropriate analogy when he asks the question, "Am I a Nee because I was born a Nee, or am I a Nee because of my behavior?" (See *The Normal Christian Life*, chapter 2.) The answer is quite obvious; he is a Nee because of his birth, not because of behavior. Romans 5:19 states, "For as through the one man's disobedience the many were made sinners . . ." Nee concludes, "I am a sinner because I am born in Adam. It is a matter not of my behavior but of my heredity, my parentage."

He then illustrates the point in a most coherent way. It is our heritage, our line of descent, that is the source of all our problems. Viewing your parental lineage as a line, where would you be today if your great-grandfather had died at the age of three? You would not be here! If an airplane in which you have placed a package crashes and is destroyed, the package has gone the way of the airplane because of its position. So it is with us; we were in Adam when he crashed!

Scripture makes the point that we are also spiritually linked to Adam, and that his sin, spiritual death, banishment from the Garden, punishment, and very nature also became ours, for we were in him from the beginning. We are born with this Adam-nature; we are what we are by birth. To our detriment, in Adam we received everything that is true of him.

We said we have tried myriad methods to change inner life by something performed in the outer life, and the end result has been nothing more than frustration and the further decline of an ugly identity that is already in need of repair. There is no way out unless we can somehow change our parentage or line of existence!

God's solution to the person with faith is complete removal of that life that was with Adam and is cut off from God, that life that is controlled by sin. He replaces it with Christ's life! As Jessie Penn-Lewis (a great teacher of cross truths) so often points out in her writings, there is only one way out of Adam, and since we came in by birth, we must go out by death. Bondage to sin came by birth; deliverance from sin comes by death. Just as in Adam we received everything that is true of him, in Christ we receive everything that is true of Christ. Once placed in His lineage, because His life is eternal we have always been in Him; therefore, when He was crucified, we were, too; when he was buried, so were we, and when He was raised and seated in heavenly places, we went with Him (now read Romans 6 with eyes of faith).

What glorious news that the "old me" I have worked so hard to change was put to death on the cross with Christ. How did all of this happen? "That no man should boast before God. But by His doing you are in Christ Jesus . . ." (I Corinthians 1:29, 30). He simply did it! It happened the day I came to Christ!

When I first began to study the teachings of the cross, I was so stirred to hope that this life of Christ could someday be mine. No less response is possible when reading such stories as *Hudson Taylor's Spiritual Secrets* and beginning to perceive what Hudson Taylor, the founder of the Inland China Mission, called the exchanged life. I wanted to experience Christ as my life, but the more I worked to experience it, the more it eluded me, because there is one thing on which God will never bend, and that one thing is faith! He will become a man to get my attention, He will overlook my sins, He will show me great compassion and mercy, but He will not do away with His demand for faith. I did not realize it, but what I was saying to God was, "If I experience Christ as my life, if I experience the crucifixion of my old self, if all my feelings of inferiority go away, then I will believe what you say." I was an unbelieving believer. Finally I said, "Lord, if I live in defeat all my life and never sense freedom from inferiority and failure, I will still believe that my old self has been crucified. I have received Christ's life, and all that is true of Him is now true of me!" Not long after that, experience followed faith.

We are sons of the most High, and once we understand who we are, we need no longer work to be that.

If I am born a Wells and one day develop amnesia and do not know who I am, does that change who I am? Of course not, but it would make me quite miserable to try to be something that I am not. Once I came to my senses and was rid of amnesia, I would find it quite natural to be a Wells, knowing that is who I really am.

Do you have amnesia? Do you know who you really are? Have you yet to come to your senses and see that because of co-crucifixion you are a child of God and can lay aside the struggle that comes from trying to change? Is it any wonder that Satan wants to blind you from this glorious truth and keep you in a state of looking to yourself to plot some way to overcome the old self?

As a believer you are completely in Christ (Romans 6:6; Ephesians 2:5, 6; Colossians 2:10). Again, the history of Christ becomes our experience and our spiritual heritage. As Nee succinctly puts it, "God has put me in Christ, and therefore all that is true of him is true of me. I will abide in him." Remember that Christian growth is merely accepting what you have always had from the first day you gave your life to Christ. Your death in Him has already taken place, so how long will you let this rotting old self remain in your house? He is, you know, beginning to smell, and no matter how you dress him up, you can no longer hide the obvious and fool your loved ones. He is dead!

Baptism is testimony to the fact and a confession of faith in what God has done (Romans 10:10). It allows you to walk in a new birth, a new life, one that you did not possess before, Christ's life, which has become your life.

We cannot say it enough: Before we can experience the fullness of His life, we must participate in the fullness of His death. Nature itself teaches us that life will come only out of death. For example, what must happen to the seed of a tree when it is planted? It must die, for not until the tiny seed is rooted in death will it begin to show its life above ground. If the seed becomes a great tree, it will only do so because it has been firmly rooted in death. So it is with Christians: We must be firmly rooted in the death of Christ before we will begin to experience His life.

For those who have discovered that this inner life in the likeness of Adam is the root of our problem, another question arises. Why, when by faith we have appropriated our death with Christ in co-crucifixion, are there still times when we find ourselves once again living in defeat? When defeat is our condition we may also be tempted to think, *The teaching does not work!* But that is impossible, simply because it is not something that we do, but rather something that God has done. It must work; it does work. It is the Holy Spirit who said, "Reckon yourselves dead to sin." God says it, not man. We are crucified with Christ whether or not we ever experience it, because God says we are! "That may be, but I still find myself once again living in defeat." Again, it is caused by seeing the cross as a one-time event, as a method, as a cure-all, and not as the moment-by-moment participation that God intends it to be to keep us near to Him.

God is not bound by something that He himself has created, such as time, and He therefore can be anywhere in time that He chooses. God can be any place at any time. In this very moment God is with the world being created, at the crucifixion of Christ, and amid the eventual destruction of the world. From His perspective, once we enter into Christ at any given point in time, we have always been in Him. "Just as He chose us in Him before the foundation of the world" (Ephesians 1:4).

Believer, you have eternal life because you have Christ's life within. You need never worry that there will come a time when God is weary of you, because you are in the very eternal life of His Son, of whom He never grows weary.

At this point, it might help if you would see Christ's life as a line that meets to form a circle, described as the Alpha and the Omega (Revelation 1:8), the first and the last (Revelation 1:17), the beginning and the end. As you view Christ's life as the eternal circle, on the line of that circle are the events of Christ's existence. Picture God in the center of the circle, turning and watching the events that take place on the line. The day that you gave your life to Christ you were brought into the line of this circle and are in Him; wherever His life is, there you are, also. As God looks to the crucifixion of His Son on the line of the circle, whom else does He see there? He sees you, for you are in Christ being crucified.

Getting into the line of this circle called eternal life was a one-time event. It happened the day you gave your life to Christ. Suppose you came to the realization in 1970 that you had been placed in the line of the circle called eternal life and therefore were crucified with Him. Now, years later, where are you? You are still in the line of the eternal life and still wherever Christ is; therefore, you are still sharing in the sufferings, the crucifixion, the burial, and the resurrection life of Jesus. Co-crucifixion is a one-time event in that it happens the moment that you enter the line of the circle, and yet it is moment by moment as you abide in His life.

Let me use the analogy of marriage. I was married once; that is, I entered into marriage on a given day. At the same time, I realize that I am married daily. If I am not experiencing marriage, where do I need to go? To my wife, of course, and why will she receive me? Is it because we married ourselves? Is it not rather on the basis of something we allowed another to do to us, which is to marry us?

If I am not experiencing the freedom that the cross is to bring from the baggage and residue of the mind left over from the old self, where do I need to go? Back to the cross! Can I go there because I crucified myself? No, but because

God placed me in Christ and I was crucified. The Christian is never to attempt self-crucifixion; it cannot be done. We are only to act on what has already been done.

Therefore, my crucifixion with Christ is an accomplished fact, but if I close the door to His life, the moment-by-moment application of the cross to my old baggage and residue—which makes the experience of the victory a reality—will cease. Again, God has structured my life to be lived in moment-by-moment fellowship with Himself.

Practical Applications of the Cross

Jesus makes an interesting statement to His disciples. In Luke 9:23, He says, "If anyone wishes to come after Me, let him deny himself, and take up his cross daily, and follow Me." There was no doubt in the disciples' minds what He was talking about. They had often witnessed someone carrying his own cross on which he would be crucified. They knew that carrying a cross was not only a testimony to all who would see that the death sentence had been given, but it also was an acknowledgment that death was deserved.

The world, sin, and Satan cry to the believer, "Save yourself! Do not take the cross!" To the degree we save our own self-lives, to that degree we spread death to those around us. But to the measure that we take up the cross, deny ourselves, and allow the cross to be applied, to that extent we will spread life to those around us.

Suppose I go home at night and my wife says to me, "I do not like the way you got mud on the rug." My attitude could be that I will not let her talk to me like that, I cannot suffer any loss at all, and who does she think she is to speak like that to me? Or I could retort, "Why does this little bit of dirt bother you? Your whole house is a pigpen!" In this way I could throw the accusations back at her, and if she, in turn, wants to suffer no loss, then the fight is on. Afterward, when we sit down to eat supper, she may fling the food on the table as we glare at one another; after a silent and hurried meal I may throw my dish in the sink and stomp off to read the newspaper or watch television. Yes, I saved myself; I did not take those demeaning remarks about my being sloppy. I showed her! I simply did not put up with it. Yes, I saved myself, but there were three little children and a wonderful wife to whom death spread because I selfishly refused the cross.

If, however, I were walking in the cross, my initial response would have been much different. I might have said, "Let me clean that up," knowing that I had nothing to save of that old Mike who was full of inferiority and had to avoid any remark that might substantiate it. He had actually been crucified with Christ. Having Christ as my new identity, I could continue to love when being accused. I might then ask her how her day went, and as we began to communicate, we would sit down to eat supper with no tension in the air, the children would be free to share the events of their day, and at the conclusion of the meal all would leave with contentment. What had happened may be unseen to all but me. I lost my life, I did not save my self, I experienced a deeper application of that one-time event of the cross, with the result being that I found myself seated in heavenly places, full of love and joy. Besides that, life has spread to three children and a wonderful wife.

I was a Bible college student when the Lord first began to impress upon me this wonderful truth. Returning from class one day, I met my wife in the kitchen. As we passed, she said something that I considered to be terribly rude. I stomped past her and went to my study to prepare for an exam. At that particular point in our marriage, I had decided that the best way to punish her was not to talk to her. The passage that needed memorizing for my test was Ephesians 5; it was not long before I reached verse 25, "Husbands, love your wives." Immediately I said, "No, Lord, not until she apologizes."

At that moment the Lord spoke to me, "Mike, go in and hug your wife and tell her you love her."

Again I responded, "No, Lord, not until she apologizes!" The Lord would not allow me to continue to study; I was stuck on verse 25. "Lord, she does not deserve it, and if I apologize now I will only encourage that kind of behavior in the future."

But the Lord spoke again, "Go and hug your wife and tell her you love her. How do you want Me to treat you when you have offended Me, Mike?"

"Oh, Lord," I said, "I want You to come to me and hug me and tell me You love me, but this is different!"

Finally, after much struggle, I submitted to my Lord and decided to make the journey into the kitchen, where I could hear my wife working. It was a very small house, but for the time and effort that the journey to the kitchen took, one might have thought that we lived in a mansion. At last I arrived. I can still picture my wife standing at that small sink, her back to me as she did the dishes. I approached her, spun her around, gave her a hug, and said, "Betty, I love you."

Her response was incredible. "Well, I am glad to see that

you finally came to your senses."

What was I to do? My worst fears were realized! I had only encouraged the behavior that I hated so much. Then the Lord spoke again, "Hug your wife again and tell her you love her." After the second hug, she simply turned around and went back to work, not saying a word. Nothing spectacular happened to her, but I was not the same. The only way that I can describe it is that it was like a branch breaking deep within me. I was losing my self-life! The cross had applied a deathblow, and I never felt more alive in my life. The lesson was not orchestrated for her, but for me! I had died that she might live. I am quite confident that I will never know until I get to heaven how much life was gained that day for my family in that little kitchen, but I can say that since that day, loving my wife has been easy. For now I do not love her because of what she does for me or to me but because of who she is. She is free from having to perform for my love, for Jesus has earned it for her.

How many Christian marriages suffer from shallow self-protectionism? How many suffer from refusing to die and keeping lists of every loss suffered at the hands of the other, watching for every word that might offend or for an encroachment on precious self? After all, "me" is all I have so I must do all that I can to protect it. Do not disagree with me, do not neglect me, be careful not to offend me, remember always to treat me with the greatest respect. The only problem that I really have is that I cannot stand me, either. Am I any the happier for all the effort it takes? Is there any contentment in demanding that everyone in the family structure life around me?

One woman came to me under the guise of wanting to save her marriage. In reality she was simply looking for someone to agree with her and make her feel good about the decision already made to leave her husband and two sons. When I would mention how the Lord might work in the situation to restore the family, she would immediately describe another of her husband's faults and assure me that the Lord could do nothing. After several minutes of jumping through hoops, I confronted her: "Who is the man?" She proceeded to tell me of the wonderful man that she had met and how much in love she was.

I explained to her an analogy that I often use to describe deception. In old horror shows there is invariably a scene wherein the monster is hiding in a closet; it is so obvious to me and everyone else in the theater that this is where he is hiding! Why, then, was the young girl in the movie moving toward the closet to open its door? Surely it must be as obvious to her as it is to the rest of us that the closet conceals the monster. Deep from within I find myself silently yelling, "Please do not open the door! The monster is in there!" The girl, who could not see what I saw, would always open the door, and by the time she realized her mistake, it was too late.

The same is true of the enemy's deceptions; others can see that the way someone is going will only lead to death and destruction, misery and loss, loneliness and pain. But it does little if any good to warn the person who is under the deep deception that behind the door he will find the answer to all his selfish desires. In the end, if the door is opened, he will recognize the deception far too late. Unfortunately, there are those who traffic in being men-pleasers, who sometimes become the worldly and so-called Christian counselors who feed false hopes for a price. Many are destroyed by them, for they only give the counsel that people want to hear. "You have wearied the Lord with your words. 'How have we wearied him?' you ask. By saying, 'All who do evil are good in the eyes of the Lord, and he is pleased with them . . .'" (Malachi 2:17 NIV).

Just so was this woman; she could not be warned. She left her husband to begin living a life of adultery, her children will no longer speak to her, and she is full of misery and loneliness. "Now therefore, thus says the Lord of hosts, 'Consider your ways! You have sown much, but harvest little; you eat, but there is not enough to be satisfied; you drink, but there is not enough to become drunk; you put on clothing, but no one is warm enough; and he who earns, earns wages to put into a purse with holes.' Thus says the Lord of hosts, 'Consider your ways!'" (Haggai 1:5-7) It is a deception to believe that self-life can ever be satisfied. Has it worked for you in the past? Are you not always left wanting more?

If you decide to retain 25 percent of your old baggage, idols, residue, and lying emotions, then that is 25 percent of the Lord that you will never know. If you decide to keep five percent of the old self, then you will be missing five percent of the Lord that you could have had. The cross of Christ is the great subtracter, and all who come in contact with it will lose many things. But all loss will be filled with an abundant measure of His presence.

To the degree that we allow the cross to apply death, to that same degree the Holy Spirit will apply life. In light of what has been said previously, listen to what Paul says: "Always carrying about in the body the dying of Jesus, that the life of Jesus also may be manifested in our body. For we who live are constantly being delivered over to death for Jesus' sake, that the life of Jesus also may be manifested in our mortal flesh. So death works in us, but life in you" (II Corinthians 4:10-12). Here is Paul's secret: He appeals to the Death/Life cycle. For we who really live, who are experiencing what Jesus promised, "I came that you might have life and have it more abundantly," are "constantly being delivered over to death."

A pastor in England once told me that we are to be the compost heaps of the world, and that if we would receive the garbage that others throw our way without refusing it, within twenty-four hours the Lord would grow something beautiful out of it. I have found this principle to stand, for every time the Lord has used me in a significant way, He has first sent a series of deathblows that brought me out of myself, caused me to open wide the door of abiding, and thus enabled me to move in His power and accomplish His supernatural intent. In spite of having learned this lesson over and over again, I cannot say that I get excited when things are going "badly" and those around me are tossing all their garbage my way, even though I know that a miracle of the Lord—for which He is preparing me to participate—is not far away. Sometimes we feel that these deathblows are going to crush us, but we must let them do just that, for it is in crushing that the precious life of the Lord encased in clay vessels is released. "But thanks be to God, who always leads us in His triumph in Christ, and manifests through us the sweet aroma of the knowledge of Him in every place. For we are a fragrance of Christ to God among those who are being saved . . ." (II Corinthians 2:14, 15).

When Christ appeared to the disciples, what was the proof of resurrection life? How did they know that He had in actual fact overcome death and the grave? How did they know it was He? "Reach here your finger, and see My hands;

and reach here your hand, and put it into My side; and be not unbelieving, but believing" (John 20:27). The proof of resurrection life will always be the marks of death. One who radiates the life of Jesus and who is a fragrant aroma will have these marks in his life. On the other hand, the one who carries the marks of self-life, boasting in ability, talents, programs, knowledge, wealth, family, or anything else from the endless list, has yet to know real life.

As I have traveled and stayed with various Christians around the world, I find the occasional Christian who is walking in all the joy and power that the Lord has for His children. As I have fellowshipped with these various brothers and sisters, I have discovered that they all have two things in common: On the one hand, they all understand the necessity of abiding moment by moment, and on the other, they all have faith. If this is an accurate perception, then surely the greatest sources of power must be prayer and abiding.

I was once traveling on an airplane when I noticed an elderly Indian woman sitting by herself, and I asked if it would be possible to sit with her. She had been a personal friend of Gandhi and began to share with me that people needed to be more humane and that there was more than one way to God. What she was saying, in essence, was that anyone who imitated Jesus would be accepted by God.

No one can imitate the Son; He must live through us. Paul instructs the Corinthians to "be imitators of me, just as I also am of Christ" (I Corinthians 11:1), and yes, we are to imitate Christ, but what is it we are to emulate? Not His work, for we cannot die for the sins of the world. We must rather copy the attitude with which He lived.

Have this attitude in yourselves which was also in Christ Jesus, who, although He existed in the form of God, did not regard equality with God a thing to be grasped, but emptied Himself, taking the form of a bond-servant, and being made in the likeness of men. And being found in appearance as a man, He humbled Himself by becoming obedient to the point of death, even death on a cross.
—Philippians 2:5-8

Imitation, following Christ as an example only, is a false teaching that was confronted by Jesus with a simple illustration of a vine, a vinedresser, and a branch. Often we find the Master Teacher using illustrations and analogies from nature, but here we find Him using such a forceful statement: "I am the true vine." He does not say He is like a vine, but rather He is the true vine! That is to say, if Jesus did not exist, neither would vines; all vines are created to teach and preach the Son of God. If we would know more of Him, then we can simply observe the vine.

One thing we can learn is "every branch in Me that does not bear fruit, He takes away; and every branch that bears fruit, He prunes it, that it may bear more fruit." I have often heard it taught that what God prunes away are those unholy things in our lives that are so displeasing to Him. Contrarily, what a vinedresser prunes from the branch are the shoots that last year bore the most fruit. That is right, the vinedresser cuts away those things that were good last year. Why does he do this? Quite simply, if the good shoots from last year are allowed to remain this year, they will require more sap (life) and produce less fruit.

This analogy points to the fact that there are legitimate programs that began under the direction of the Lord and produced great fruit for the body of Christ, but sometimes those who initiated the program became so enamored with the end result that they later refused to allow the Lord to prune. They placed trust in the program instead of in God. Many ministries that began twenty years ago on just such a blessing from the Lord now resist the operation of the Vinedresser and, as a result, take twenty times the energy and produce twenty times less fruit.

The key element in the whole process that is forgotten is that the fruit borne was the result of abiding; when these believers were abiding, the Lord was able to implement His program. But the enemy got their eyes off abiding, so that they would believe the great blessing was the result of the procedure God introduced. Cutting away what was a blessing last year enables believers to maintain the focus on Him and allows Him to bring whatever is needed this year. The need today is the same as the need in the past—Jesus—but the methods by which God reaches mankind continue to change. All that is needed for success will come as we abide in Him moment by moment, and it will come no other way.

The enemy continues efforts to have our eyes rest upon the wrong things. We are not to focus on the results of abiding, and in so doing cease to abide, but we are always to have our eyes on Him, which will produce fruit. Is this how John 15:2 reads to you? "Every branch in Me that does not pray each day, attend church, read his Bible, have an inspirational marriage, have pure thoughts, stop cursing, become a bold witness, have great emotional experiences, and have a full-time ministry He takes away." No! Our one purpose in life is to bear fruit, not to do something for the Lord.

When I was in Australia, a woman came to me at the end of one of the conferences. She said that she had really enjoyed the lectures and had also attended the year before. What she wanted to say was that even though she enjoyed being there, she wanted me to know that it did not work. I am always interested in such comments, because abiding has to work; there is nothing for us to do, since it is God who does everything. I asked her to explain further. She described how she had been in therapy to stop overeating. It was a problem that she had been plagued with for many years, and she had tried everything—books, group therapy, hypnotism, hospitalization, and, of course, my seminar. She then asked, "What should I do?"

The answer was really quite simple: "Go home and eat!"

She stared at me and said, "You do not mean it!"

I responded, "I do mean it; go home and eat." I then explained to her that if she could deliver herself from overeating she already would have; if I could deliver her I would. Therefore, each morning I wanted her to get up and say, "Lord, apart from You I can do nothing. I give You my overeating, and I thank You that no matter what, You have taken it," and then go eat. I soon heard from her that she was no longer overeating! Why? It was simply because her eyes were no longer on food, but on the Lord who supplies a life that has overcome bondage.

On one occasion a cocaine addict, who had been an unbeliever, came to me for consultation. One day after he had given his life to the Lord, he asked, "What am I to do with my addiction?"

I first asked if he was certain that he wanted to lose his addiction, and he assured me that he was. I then said, "We will pray and give the addiction to God, allowing Him to have it." He agreed, and we prayed. Afterward, he asked what he was to do that night when he normally would begin to crave cocaine. My response was to go ahead and take it, but that each morning he was to pray before he even got out of bed, "Lord, apart from You I can do nothing; today I give You my cocaine addiction, and I thank You that no matter what, You have taken it." Anybody can be commanded not to take cocaine. This man was not an idiot; he did not want to take the drug, and if he could quit he already would have! What was needed was the supernatural action of God that comes only when we have our eyes off the problem and on Him through abiding.

The man called me three days later to tell me what had transpired since I saw him. The first morning he had prayed as instructed and gone ahead and taken the cocaine. On the second morning he did the same, but on the third morning after praying he simply could not pick up the needle! He was elated, and why not? He had been supernaturally delivered by the very hand of the living God. Praise Him!

The Lord has delivered me from all sorts of manifestations of the flesh, but not one time has He delivered me when I had my eyes focused on them. There have been times when I was so vexed by a particular problem that I decided to read, study, and overcome. Alas, all that ever came from that was more severe defeat! Only when I have been in an abiding relationship has the Lord delivered me from those problems, and I usually never noticed until sometime later that they had naturally fallen aside.

If you are focused on your troubles right now, you will not find deliverance. The Vine is always to have first place. "I am the vine, you are the branches; he who abides in Me, and I in him, he bears much fruit; for apart from Me you can do nothing" (John 15:5).

Just as a branch has no life within itself, Christians are not called to generate life, but to receive it. We are not called to imitate the life of Christ, but to participate in it. When we learn the abiding life, we will find ourselves doing by very nature the things so many struggle and work for years to accomplish, because we have the same fiber, the same life, and the same Spirit as the Vine, being one with it!

My mother has always kept very beautiful imitation fruit on her dining room table. On more than one occasion I have tried to sneak a piece of fruit, only to be reminded that it is inedible. If we were to visit the factory that produced the imitation fruit, we would find the machinery running there quite noisy and hot, emitting a very unpleasant odor. By contrast, if we were to visit a vineyard, we would want to have with us a blanket and a nice pillow and lay them between the rows of grapevines. We could lie down in the cool shade of the vines, enjoy the pleasant odors, and listen to the peaceful surroundings as the grapes grew. There is quite a difference between the machinery that works to produce an imitation of life and the vine that produces life.

We find a corresponding dissimilarity between the Christian who imitates and the one who abides. Those who work are noisy and feverish; their efforts do not produce a sweet-smelling aroma to the Lord. Their fruit, which often will fool others at first glance, will be found merely to be counterfeit. But the believer who has learned the secret of abiding is quiet, refreshing, and full of real life, Christ's life! He has fragrant, revitalizing fruit produced not for himself but for others to enjoy, that they might be renewed and live. His life is spontaneous; he never emphasizes doing but abiding, and his eyes do not stray from his precious Vine. He has no worries, for the Vinedresser and the Vine take care of everything. He submits to pruning readily, for he knows it brings greater closeness with God and more abundant life. The branch acknowledges with joy, "Apart from You I can do nothing."

"Dear Father, we praise and thank You for the life of the Vine. Today, in this moment, we choose to abide and thus allow You to fill us with the precious life of Your Son, the True Vine."

The Moment-by-Moment Work of His Blood

In the Old Testament, man's complaint against God was that He did not understand what it was like to be a man, while God's complaint was that man did not know what it was like to be a holy and just God. God's solution was to send the God/man, Jesus Christ, the Word become flesh (born of a woman). This Jesus would be the great intercessor for God to man and man to God, for He could understand and sympathize with both, being Intercessor and High Priest, King and Lord, Brother and Mediator. He was God in a man's body with a man's soul. Satan tempted the human Jesus, but the divine Spirit within refused all temptation, and therefore the Spirit of God in a human body destroyed the works of Satan. We are told that Jesus was tempted in all things! I am not sure how long it must take to be tempted in all things, but I believe I would be safe to assume that it would take a little over thirty-three and a half years.

At the point of Christ's death the Spirit had overcome every one of our enemies in a body and soul just like ours! If somehow I could get that precious Spirit and place it in my human body and soul, I would be completely victorious! In fact, if I could release that Spirit that has already overcome all the enemies of a human, the end result would be that of which Jesus spoke in John, "Truly, truly, I say to you, he who believes in Me, the works that I do shall he do also; and *greater works* than these shall he do; because I go to the Father" (John 14:12, emphasis mine).

The secret is found in the blood of Christ. Is that not why the New Testament mentions blood over ninety times? The blood of Jesus is a most precious thing; unfortunately, most only understand its excellence from the standpoint of the forgiveness of sins and being kept from hell in the future. They see the blood as something of value in the past and in the future but have not considered its present worth. Any ignorance of the daily work of the blood in defeating all the enemies that man has is one of Satan's prized accomplishments, for the blood released in our life moment by moment means secured victory over every temptation, lying emotion, fear, frustration, and any other enemy.

Eternal life—Christ's life—has no beginning or end, and God, not being bound by time, can move to any point in time right now. Therefore, what eternal life accomplishes once, it also accomplishes moment by moment. Once God does something in eternity, it is always being done. This blood possesses that indestructible quality, the vitality that has torn the veil top to bottom, and the life that is obedient to the Father, is full of all the esteemed fruit, is not self-pleasing, and possesses the very nature of Jesus!

The cross and its resulting blood cannot be separated; both have a one-time effect and a moment-by-moment consequence on our lives. I was crucified with Christ once on the day I received Him, but placed in His eternal life I am now crucified always. I was forgiven and restored by the blood of Jesus the day I received Him as Savior, but once in his eternal life, I am delivered moment by moment by His precious blood. The blood of Christ was not given without the sacrifice of self, nor will it be received without the sacrifice of myself at the cross of Christ.

Let me explain it this way. Suppose I purchased a very old truck with the intent of rebuilding it. When I made the acquisition I was sure that very little effort and money would have to be expended for restoration, but as the work progressed I found more and more wrong and spent a greater and greater amount of money. The more I fixed, the more the vehicle seemed to break. One day as I worked, I finally became sick of it and decided to take my losses; I wanted nothing more to do with it. I called a wrecker and asked him to tow it away. When the garage was empty, I still had one memento: my hands were dirty! If I wanted no more remembrance of the truck or proof that I once owned it, I would have to wash my hands!

Think of that truck as your old Adam-life that you tried so hard to change until you decided to have it taken away by co-crucifixion. However, the pollution of that old life still remains in your mind, habits, and desires. You now need the blood of Jesus to cleanse all those old contaminants away, and as you open the door of abiding and allow the blood to flow, even the remembrance of these things will go. The blood takes away the feeling of defilement that sin brings. "But if we walk in the light as He Himself is in the light, we have fellowship with one another, and the blood of Jesus His Son cleanses us from all sin" (I John 1:7). This cleansing that the blood accomplishes takes away every hindrance that we might have and creates in us a pure heart.

In the temple, the Holy of Holies where God dwelt was protected by a thick veil, behind which the priest could go only once a year after blood was spilt. The veil represented the reign of the old Adam-life; as long as it remained, the presence of God was denied to you. The day that Jesus was crucified and you were in Him, the veil was rent in two. The presence of God is now accessible to you, but only with the blood of Jesus, which you possess; because of its immense value and eternal power, it allows admission not once a year but every moment. All you need do is bow before God and enter in "with boldness" by the power of His blood.

Again, and we cannot hear it enough, since the blood possesses an eternal life (that is, a life that never diminishes in power), then what the blood accomplished once it continues to accomplish. What, then, did and does the blood achieve for the children of God? Redemption and forgiveness, Ephesians 1:7; sanctification, Hebrews 13:12; fellowship, Ephesians 2:13; total commitment, Revelation 5:9; confidence and the presence of God, Hebrews 10:19-21; heaven held open for us, Hebrews 9:12; overcoming of death and the grave, Hebrews 13:20; justification, Romans 3:24, 25; peace, Colossians 1:20; and the overcoming of Satan, Revelation 12:11. Do you see the beauty of the blood?

Now stop one moment and dwell on the precious blood of Jesus, on the merit of which at this moment you have access to the Father. You stand making requests not on the basis of your attainments but on the success of His blood. The blood of Jesus is so precious to the Father that He will not refuse you; actually, He expects you to take full advantage of this costly flow, never letting one drop be wasted; He wants the blood maximized. This is not to say, "Sin so grace will abound," but to affirm that the blood is so costly that the Father and the Son want the Christian to experience every possible benefit that can come from it.

In the mountains my wife and I have a small cabin on which we make monthly payments. At times it is a sacrifice to make the payments, and all too often we are not able to spend much time there. However, when we cannot be there but some of our brothers and sisters in Christ go relax, enjoy God's creation, and spend time with the Lord and their families, we receive a different kind of satisfaction that is vicarious but nonetheless real. The cabin that is not directly benefitting us gives pleasure to others, and that makes the monthly payments enjoyable.

The same is true with the blood of Christ, the payment for which was great. God receives pleasure when we take advantage of what cost Him so much. Are you afraid of making requests to the Father? If you are, I fear it is because your request is based on your merit, not the value of the blood. Can you be as bold in making an appeal when you have failed God as you are when you have been a success? If not, then your standing is not based on the blood but on your own perceived righteousness. When you have failed, enter boldly before the Father and you will discover just how precious this blood is to Him. Once you understand the unparalleled worth of the blood, you will find yourself always before Him with confidence.

One early morning I received a call from my mother stating that my grandfather was in the hospital. Since I am very close to him, the enemy had a perfect opportunity to whisper in my ear, "If only you were closer to God, if only you had been praying more, if only you had spent more time in the Scripture, then in your time of need you could enter into the presence of God and He would hear you." For just a moment I gave ground to those thoughts before realizing that they neglected the blood of Jesus; if access to the Father were based on my stature, then Christ would not have had to come. With great joy I approached the Father in heaven "in whom we have boldness and confident access through faith in Him"—Ephesians 3:12. "Since therefore, brethren, we have confidence to enter the holy place by the blood of Jesus" (Hebrews 10:19), the believer does not operate under the world's system of performance-based acceptance, but under Christ-based acceptance.

How to Live the Abiding Life

I am reminded of the young fish that said to the old fish, "I long to someday see the great ocean."

The old fish looked with amazement and stated, "You are right now in the great ocean!"

The young fish responded, "What? I don't see any great ocean." You see, the young fish could not recognize it, for he had a preconceived notion of what it would be like. He would continue to look for that wonderful place, not knowing that all along he dwelt in it!

Abiding in Christ is often viewed by many in the same way; they are waiting to see and feel it before they will believe it, while all along they have been in that relationship and most blessed existence.

One of my brothers in India tells the story of how he came to Christ in an abiding relationship through a Hindu guru. My friend grew up wanting more than anything else to be a medical doctor, and to that end he studied seriously. The day he was to register in medical school he became quite sick and, consequently, was a day late for enrollment. Upon arrival the next day he was informed that the medical school was filled and the only course of instruction that he would be offered was in botany. As you can well imagine, he was very disappointed. Nevertheless, he applied himself diligently to his studies and in time became a professor. All during this period he was an unbeliever.

One day while taking his students on a field trip in the jungle, he noticed a very old Hindu man get up from a small shrine, hobble to a fast stream, wade out to the middle, take a bath, and return. This event stirred his curiosity, since his own young students were not even able to ford the rapidly flowing stream. He went to the old man to ask how he was able to accomplish such a thing, and while speaking he realized that the old man was also blind, which made the whole scenario even more fascinating. The old man described his success in the water as follows: "I have a stick that I use to guide me. I put my stick down ahead of me; if the ground is firm, I feel around the stick with my foot, place my foot where the stick is, and know that I am safe. I then move the stick and do the same. I follow my stick. I go where the stick takes me, for I know it will keep me safe. I followed the stick into the water and followed it safely out." My friend thanked the old man and began to walk away, when the old man called him back, saying, "I am not finished. The problem with your generation is that you do not have a stick." That vexed my friend. He was going through life without a stick! He had nothing to lead him, nothing to tell him where to put his foot, nothing to follow to safe ground.

A few days later he looked on his bookshelf and saw a Bible; out of desperation he opened it. To what do you suppose the pages fell open for this unbelieving botanist without a stick to carry him through life?

I am the true vine, and My Father is the vinedresser. Every branch in Me that does not bear fruit, He takes away; and every branch that bears fruit, He prunes it, that it may bear more fruit. You are already clean because of the word which I have spoken to you. Abide in Me, and I in you. As the branch cannot bear fruit of itself, unless it abides in the vine, so neither can you, unless you abide in Me. I am the vine, you are the branches; he who abides in Me, and I in him, he bears much fruit; for apart from Me you can do nothing.

—John 15:1-5

Can you imagine all the impact that this verse had on the searching plant specialist? He knew that the vine and the branch became one, that the fiber of the vine became the fiber of the branch; he knew that the life of the vine became the very life of the branch, and he knew so well that the branch in and of itself could do nothing! Praise God! He had found his stick; he now had Someone to guide him and show him where to place each foot; he was safe. Is it not just like our God to design his being a botanist rather than a medical doctor and to convict him of his lost state through a man who was lost himself? Oh, how this brother testifies to the abundance of living the abiding life, the simplest life to live, not maintained by struggle, but given by God.

The "how-to" of abiding begins not with a work, but with an attitude to be maintained. We live in an attitude of abiding, deeply aware that Christ is our life. First, we are to be constantly mindful of our true condition were we to be outside of the Vine. There are very few today who can actually say that they know themselves, but we must undergo this very unpleasant process. The Apostle Peter is a classic example of someone who did not know himself. He could make such confident assertions as, "I will never deny You, Lord," and yet that was the very thing he did. He did not know himself.

Take a teenager who assures you that he can go to the party and not give in to the peer pressure to take drugs and drink, or that she can have a boyfriend and not become sexually involved. Such statements tell you immediately that this person cannot be trusted, for he or she does not know him- or herself.

Coming to know oneself and accepting the fact that in one's body dwells no good thing is not easy, and often this is accompanied by much suffering. However, once the lesson is learned, Paul's command will be gladly received. "Have this attitude in yourselves which was also in Christ Jesus, who, although He existed in the form of God, did not regard equality with God a thing to be grasped, but emptied Himself, taking the form of a bondservant . . ." (Philippians 2:5-7). The first step, then, is to know ourselves and carry the attitude of absolute dependence that comes from this knowledge throughout the day.

Second, each of us must take his place as one who believes. Believing is not so much work as it is rest, not so much activity as it is receiving, and not so much what is immediately reaped as patience in the wait prior to obtaining. Faith is waiting on God to provide in quiet confidence, something that every living creature fathoms except man, who must learn it. Faith is enjoyable waiting and easy resting. What makes it so enjoyable and easy, you might ask. We know that God provides for what He has created. Does a branch have ulcers from worrying about the care that the vine will give it? Never! It rests in its position, trusting the responsibility of the vine and never trying to do its job! The believer standing in faith will rest as a creature who does not take upon himself the function of the Creator. Our second attitude, then, has to do with faith. We understand that if abiding is dependent upon us it is impossible, but we have courage, for we have learned that it is God who keeps us.

Third, we are aware that the abiding life is not a feeling but an awareness. One of the great secrets of the Christian life is that when one is filled with the Spirit he generally feels nothing, since it is the natural and normal way of life. Just as a branch feels nothing out of the ordinary when receiving sap from the vine, the abiding believer is aware of his position in quiet confidence, not toiling but yielding to His work and knowing he is being kept! Abiding involves knowing that He is keeping us even when we cannot keep ourselves.

Fourth, we take our place as the creatures and give up our tendency and desire to play the role of the Creator. We understand that we are His creation and with full confidence expect Him to maintain us. We see that the abiding life is only possible because He who calls us will lead us to and keep us in it. Often we can come to this conviction only after we have tried and failed at abiding by our own efforts.

Once we have taken our place as the creatures, next we resolve to live only one moment at a time. This is a most difficult accomplishment; we are so accustomed to thinking of yesterday and then tomorrow, not knowing that yesterday is past and tomorrow belongs to God. Can we see that there is nothing that we can do to provide for tomorrow, since this moment is all that we have?

Nor is it good to look forward to tomorrow. Imagine that you are handed a book on how to build a computer and told to get started. The worst thing that you could do would be to turn to the last page and gaze at the finished product. Without following each step of assembly, you would easily be discouraged by looking at the completed computer and would most likely quit before you began.

Imagine, too, a book that tells your whole life story. What would happen if you turned to the middle of the book and there read that you would lose a child in the future? Once you read such a thing, it would not be possible to concentrate on daily life, nor would you be able to enjoy the child today. This event in the future would steal every moment from you until the day that the child died. However, if you refuse to look ahead to that chapter, but rather take your life one page at a time, day by day and moment by moment lived in the presence of the Lord, you would find that when that day in the future comes, you would have all the grace needed to see you through the calamity. We creatures are too easily overwhelmed by any more than one day. "Therefore do not be anxious for tomorrow; for tomorrow will care for itself. Each day has enough trouble of its own" (Matthew 6:34).

Life is only to be lived one moment at a time, being faithful in each to experience His life. God will then give succeeding moments wherein we are abiding and full of His life, and these moments will soon turn into days, and finally into a lifetime of living out of the joy of the Master's presence. The future belongs to God! Ask only for the grace that you need today as you speak to the rebellious child, when you must work at a job you do not like, today as you desire to make your marriage a blessing, as you attempt to share with a lost one, and as you wish to live in an abiding relationship with our Lord.

These are the attitudes needed to experience the abiding life. Once we possess these, we will know that abiding does not depend on our strength, growth, feelings, failures, or success, but on His ability to place us in the Vine and keep us there. Each day can begin with this simple confession: "This day, Lord, I thank You that I am in You and You are in me. Thank You that no matter how I feel, I abide in You. Thank You, Lord, that it is not a position I must struggle to maintain, for You have put me there. This moment is all I will be concerned for. I accept my position of abiding with joy."

Chapter 9
Freedom to Fail

The only way out of failure is faith. We do not wallow in self-pity and guilt, but we allow failure to bring us to a place of true dependence, which will bring maximum productivity as Christ lives His life through us. Regrets are for unbelievers, not for those who walk in Christ's righteousness.

When we fail we must understand the character of God that causes all things to work together for good. In comprehending His character, there is one secret that all who serve Him should learn: His very nature is compassion. The repentant man, no matter how far he has fallen, can count on God's hearing him and being overcome by His own compassion!

Israel was warned that if she forgot the Lord and worshiped idols she would be destroyed, but if when in distress from that behavior she would seek the Lord, then God would hear her. "For the Lord your God is a compassionate God; He will not fail you nor destroy you . . ." (Deuteronomy 4:31). In the Book of Hosea, God presents His charge against Israel: They are unfaithful, unrepentant, wicked, rebellious, idolatrous, deceived, and defiled. Therefore, they must come under His judgment and be broken, oppressed, cut off, childless, enslaved, devastated, and rejected. But listen to what God says: "How can I give you up, Ephraim? How can I hand you over, Israel? How can I treat you like Admah? How can I make you like Zeboiim? My heart is changed within me;

all my *compassion* is aroused. I will not carry out my fierce anger, nor will I turn and devastate Ephraim. *For I am God, and not man*—the Holy One among you. I will not come in wrath" (Hosea 11:8, 9 NIV, italics added). We are free to fail because God is a God of compassion; over sixty times in the Old Testament is He described thus.

It was the compassion of God that so upset the prophet Jonah; he knew that God would not destroy Nineveh if they repented. Jonah believed that Nineveh should be annihilated even if they did repent; their wrongs should not be overlooked! "Oh, Lord, is this not what I said when I was still at home? That is why I was so quick to flee to Tarshish. I knew that you are a gracious and compassionate God, slow to anger and abounding in love, a God who relents from sending calamity" (Jonah 4:2 NIV). Our Father cannot overlook a repentant heart, no matter how severe the sin.

One thing that we see over and over again is what I call God's Compassion Cycle. That is, whenever we are punished by God, our resulting suffering stirs His compassion, so He brings us back again to Himself. "For the Lord will not reject forever, for if He causes grief, then He will have compassion according to His abundant lovingkindness" (Lamentations 3:31, 32).

What is your excuse for wallowing? To what end or benefit do you continue to punish yourself because of unbelief after you have sinned? God is compassionate, whether you believe it or not. His character is not dependent upon what you believe or feel, but on what He says. King David himself, when given the choice between having God or man mete out his punishment, chose God, from whom he knew he could find compassion. Have you learned to lean on the compassion of God, or do your lying emotions tell you God does not hear and show compassion?

God continued to forgive and restore Israel even though He knew that they would continue to fail and not keep their promises to Him. It is the compassion of God that has brought all of us thus far. There have been countless times when we have told God we would do better, and although we fully intended to, we simply did not. We cannot continue to believe that God wants to hear us say we will improve before He restores us to His presence; He actually wants us to come to Him in weakness and humility, not in the feigned strength of what we think we can accomplish.

For those of us who have experienced the compassion of God, is it any wonder that He commands us, "And so, as those who have been chosen of God, holy and beloved, put on a heart of compassion, kindness, humility, gentleness, and patience; bearing with one another, and forgiving each other, whoever has a complaint against anyone; just as the Lord forgave you, so also should you" (Colossians 3:12, 13)? We who know the compassion of the Lord must show the same to others. No matter how often someone has failed, we must show mercy, understand the weakness of the person with whom we are dealing, and realize that if our lives had gone as his had we might not even be faring as well as he is. Compassion readily forgives.

There are great promises for those who show love and mercy in snatching someone from defeat. ". . . love covers a multitude of sins" (I Peter 4:8). ". . . mercy triumphs over judgment" (James 2:13), and "he who turns a sinner from the error of his way will save his soul from death, and will cover a multitude of sins" (James 5:20). When we walk in compassion, we are free to fail, our love covers a multitude of our sins, and our mercy delivers us from judgment. God has truly done everything possible to make this life of ours abundant.

CHAPTER 10
The Deeper Work Of the Enemy

As we begin to live out our life in Christ, experiencing the deeper walk that abiding in Him yields, the works of the enemy correspondingly intensify. No longer will he use the obvious and overt (lust, gossip, slander, and all worldly desire) to turn us away from Christ, but rather sly new attacks consisting of well-placed lies (99 percent truth) to thwart the production of so much fruit.

Often I have commented to struggling Christians that we will know if we have truly hit on the answer to their defeat by how hard the enemy will work in the coming weeks to take them out of the abiding life. I have frequently watched him unleash everything at his disposal to drive a brother or sister back to the state of saving self, denying the cross, and unbelief in order to keep that one from abiding in the truth. Basically, we know that we are moving in the right direction if things get worse before they get better. A person moving in a falsehood that will not bring deliverance will be greatly encouraged by Satan along the way. Those who are on the path of do's (seeking God's acceptance by performance) will likewise be urged along, while those on the path of believing will find many obstacles.

When it comes to the enemy, it is God's will that we stand against him in the victory that is ours in Christ. Satan's tactic is either to have us disregard him, treating him as though he does not exist (fall short of the will of God), or be consumed with fighting against him (going beyond the will of God). We must see that Satan is alive and very active, our adversary (I Peter 5:8) against whom we battle, with his many schemes (Ephesians 6:11) and snares (II Timothy 2:26), and we must all take heed lest we fall (I Corinthians 10:12).

Satan is, of course, a great liar and the father of lies (John 8:44). We will now turn our attention to some of his most significant lies, which are most subtle and therefore most dangerous.

Satan Has Not Been Stripped of His Power?

Many have fallen for the lie that Jesus has not stripped Satan of his power. "I was watching Satan fall from heaven like lightning" (Luke 10:18). Once Christ as our life is accepted by faith, we will begin to take an offensive position against the enemy, refusing the lie that he has more power than we do in Christ and exercising the release of the life within us that has already defeated Satan at every turn.

In conjunction with this deception, many are told that when there is something in their lives they cannot overcome, they should seek the Lord to see if there might be some type of demon dwelling within them. Though there is no scriptural basis for a demon's inhabiting a believer, this will be taught with fierceness because of what has been seen or heard. Often, in spite of deep commitment to Christ and a desire to be pleasing, an otherwise capable teacher will become accustomed to neglecting the fact that something he is imparting cannot be found in Scripture.

Again, the issue is to find what works in terms of being conducive to a victorious Christian walk. I have discipled many believers who have gone through the nightmare of having demons with a variety of names and sources cast from them. This type of contrived deliverance will often bring a temporary emotional relief, which is entangling in that this is then often viewed as the answer, and subjection to darkness will increase. But in the end, when problems recur, these believers are then told they did not struggle hard enough to keep the demons out, which avoids the real issue that the whole process did not work. The frightening thing about this teaching is that it takes a Christian's mind off the light of God and directs his eyes toward the darkness of Satan. Once a believer is persuaded that he can be possessed by demons (whether in body, soul, or spirit; Scripture never tells us what part of an unbeliever the demon does inhabit), he opens himself up to all manner of deceptions and manifestations of Satan. The enemy loves this kind of doubt and turmoil.

If Satan is able to possess Christians as easily as many report, is it not reasonable to assume he could wreak much more havoc than we now see? He could possess many airline pilots, causing crashes and much death, or the men who watch over nuclear bomb sites. Why does Satan not do such things, given his nature? The answer must be quite simple: he cannot! But he can lie and deceive and make Christians waste time casting demons out of one another, not standing against him with heavenly power to accomplish the true work of the Kingdom.

Even the Old Testament teaches that an evil spirit cannot enter the one who has God's Spirit; the Spirit of the Lord must first leave before an evil spirit (with God's permission) can penetrate (I Samuel 16:14). We know from the Book of Job that Satan does not touch the elect without the permission of God, and in Jesus' prayer (which He established was heard and answered) we are ensured protection, not because of the life we live, but the life He lived. ". . . I come to Thee, Holy Father, keep them in Thy name, the name which Thou hast given Me, that they may be one, even as We are . . . I do not ask Thee to take them out of the world, but to keep them from the evil one" (John 17:11, 15). "Greater is He who is in you than he who is in the world."

Church history does not bear out that casting demons out of Christians was ever a solution to defeat. It does, however, bear out that the enemy has continually introduced one-time solutions into the Church, all calculated to keep our eyes off of Jesus. If demons are so much the problem, why is it that Paul and the other writers of the New Testament neglected to come right out and tell us so? Instead, Scriptures are often twisted and manipulated to fit the experience of believers, some of whom even claim to have received their teaching about demons from demons, not at all a reputable or reliable source (I Timothy 4:1)!

This is not to say that a Christian cannot be oppressed; we know that does occur. All too often what the enemy uses to harass the believer are particular manifestations of the flesh; these, as we have already mentioned, are removed by taking up the cross daily, which will cut the ground out from under the enemy and free us from his influence. It would almost be wonderful if our problems were simply demons that could be cast out to give us that one-time remedy. Again, the defeated are found even among the teachers who traffic in such procedures.

If Christ in you cannot keep demons from dwelling in you, what chance do you have of keeping them out? Victory belongs not to those who try to generate power over the enemy, but to those who receive Christ's power.

(Note: See Heb. 2:14; I Jn. 5:18; Rm. 12:1, 8:14, 6:6 & 13, 8:23; I Peter 1:5; II Tim. 4:18; Col. 1:13, 29; I Cor. 3:6, 6:11, 19, & 20, 7:34, 10:20, 21; Gal. 6:8; Acts 26:18)

I Must Work To Be What God Says I Am By Birth?

One of the Brazilian brothers pointed out to me that when Adam and Eve were tempted to be like God, they were already made in the image of God. In a like manner, Christ was tempted in the wilderness to prove that He was God, when in fact He was already God. Just so is it with us; the enemy will continue to tempt us to work to become what we already are. Once we succumb to this temptation, we cast aside faith as well as walking as who God says we are, and we give in to unbelief.

Closely linked to this lie is another which says, "The carnal life is all that I can live." Remember that Satan's voice will always sound like a believer's own. The enemy will rarely give up on his attempts to brainwash the Christian. He never wants us to realize who we are in Christ, for in so doing we will take an offensive position against him, entering into the battle to take from him those whom he has worked so hard to hold captive. The truth is that believers never have to live a carnal life or place their will under his power; we can choose to abide in Christ.

To Possess I Must Experience?

Many are working to have oneness with the Lord or oneness in their marriages, when in fact oneness is something that is given, not worked for. Experience must come out of faith, which is the "conviction of things not yet seen." Because we have not experienced all does not mean that we do not possess all. If the experience never comes, still we will believe what He has spoken. The other side of this problem is that the enemy would like to define for us what the experience should be and have us believe that until we have those feelings he specifies, we do not possess what God has given us.

Take, for example, the whole issue of knowing whether a person is going to heaven. Many have allowed the enemy to define for them what this assurance will feel like, such as a great emotional release, visions, appointments, the list being as varied as are the believers. We must remember that our assurance is based on what God tells us, not anything else. John 3:16 simply says, "Whoever believes," period. Once again, the enemy will always add to God's simple statements, just as he did when speaking to Eve in the Garden.

There are those who are so governed by emotion that the worst thing that the Lord could do upon their first accepting Him would be to give them an emotional experience, for in so doing, God would be encouraging them to continue to be led by emotion. For this type of person it would be important to have no emotional experience and to learn to walk by faith without feeling. The experience that God gives each individual will always be just the one needed.

We must also be careful to allow all experiences to transpire without trying to force them, because the enemy (sometimes by way of other believers) may have defined a particular experience as our assurance. Know this, that one sure sign of assurance is questioning the fact of being born again.

We must be careful to allow only God to define what is ours in Christ and not allow the enemy to add qualifiers. We also must not allow the enemy to define what a successful believer is, because it will so often have to do with accomplishing something great for the Lord; his logic is characteristically, "If I can do something great for the Lord, then He will be pleased, and I will gain His favor and acceptance." Such a thought has its roots in hell, for it denies the Christian's standing before the Father by faith in Christ's work, not his own. Nowhere are we commended for doing the great thing; rather, the emphasis is on faithfulness in the smallest of things: for the child, in such as obedience; for the wife, simple respect for her husband; and for the husband, loving his wife. Successful Christianity involves forgiving, loving the unlovable, giving instead of storing up treasures on earth, and abiding in Him. We must always allow God to specify what Christianity is, and we will find that it is rarely what we think it is.

The Confusion Over Where the True Battle Is

The enemy would never have us fighting the battle where the frontlines actually exist; he will always bring something to our attention that has nothing to do with the real issue. Many continue to respond to the negative statements of their mates, believing that logic and reason will prevail. They believe that their present problem is due to misunderstanding or wrong thinking, and if only they can appeal to reason and make a good case for their side of the argument, then there will be agreement and harmony. In so doing, the believer will more often than not be fighting a person rather than the enemy who inspires the false thoughts that are emanating from the person.

Imagine that you are in a war zone, trapped in a foxhole and unable to look above it. Your only course of action is to throw hand grenades out, hoping that they will hit the enemy. Would it not be wonderful if for a time everyone in the battle were to be frozen while a hot air balloon descended and took you above the battle, showed you the position of the enemy, and then placed you back in the foxhole before the battle resumed? In the midst of spiritual battle, take time with God; allow the realization of your being "seated with Him in the heavenlies"; let Him show you where the proper battle lines are, so that knowing the position of the enemy you will no longer be wasting your energies.

There is another problem with not fighting the battle on the proper line: We can unknowingly aid the enemy in his work to destroy other believers. When someone is acting in a way that is unpleasing to the Lord and we continue to bring it to his attention, what are we doing? We intensify the problem by helping the enemy place the person's eyes on something other than the solution. If we want a loving husband, a loving wife, an obedient child, honest employees, a respectful employer, a faithful friend, and a spiritual pastor, what must be done? The only hope that we have is to place their eyes on the Savior who can deliver them from vexing behavior. None will find deliverance anywhere else save in Christ.

As we choose to fight the battle on the proper battle line, we recognize that the problems we see around us are manifestations of life void (at least in the present moment) of abiding. We will then join the struggle to see those around us abide, and in this way the problems will disappear.

Total Surrender Will Bring Pain and Loss?

Will total surrender bring pain and loss? Actually, the opposite is true: The lack of total surrender will bring pain and loss! The enemy invests great energy in this lie.

It is whispered continually to the growing believer who has given up all but one thing to serve the Lord, that one thing which is coveted, which has brought pleasure, which allows independence, and that allows the enemy to maintain a foothold in the believer's life. What is this one thing? It differs among Christians but will generally have to do with some right which we believe we should have: a right to be in control, not to forgive, to keep that one idol, or to have some kind of worldly possession or pleasure. For the person who wants more than anything to serve God and be pleasing, it is important that any one claim never be brought to the forefront but remain hidden away from sight, rarely thought about; nevertheless, it is the one thing he feels he must have. Because past satisfaction was derived from this one thing, it is continually protected and justified. It is, of course, a paradox, for the one thing has also brought continual misery; the enemy can continue to make life miserable as he fights to turn this foothold into a sizeable piece of property and then a stronghold. However, since this particular type of believer has given up all else, the enemy is rarely successful in his attempts to gain a stronghold, but he uses this one thing to take the edge off the person's walk with the Lord and keep him away from the full experience of joy.

It reminds me of being in a cabin in the mountains, where it is perfectly peaceful and absolutely beautiful until my rest is disturbed by one small fly buzzing around my head, landing, biting, and annoying! All of the grandeur of the great mountains is destroyed for me by one small fly.

So it is with this one small thing; it never quite allows us to enjoy all that God has given because of its nagging presence. We see it in marriages where the enemy whispers,

"If you give in to him, you will become a doormat." "If you love her now, you will only be encouraging her behavior." The couples in this deception, each holding on to his or her right to be in control, lying in bed refusing to touch the other, and declining to communicate, forfeit abundant life. They have pain and loss because they do not have total surrender.

When it comes to taking up the cross and denying self-life residue, the lies will take this form: "You must wait for others to die to self-life and abide before you do." "If you deny yourself you will not be happy." "Denial of self leads to abuse by others." "I will do it if my mate will do it." These are deep deceptions, for if the Lord is calling you to self-denial, He is calling you to abundant life. Since you have heard the message of abiding, you are to be the first to deny self and, therefore, the first to experience the blessing.

These lies are built upon the one Paul confronts in the Book of Philemon. Paul knows that making an appeal for the release of Onesimus based on his past history is ridiculous. He therefore makes his appeal on the basis of Paul's own treatment of Philemon and the handling that Philemon has received from the Lord.

The kind of forgiveness, love, submission, and respect toward others which the Lord requires of us will never come if based on their actions. The Lord makes such demands on the basis of how He has treated us, not how others have acted. We are commanded to love because of the intensity with which He has loved us. The very thought that others do not deserve love because of their behavior is hellish and demonic, and those who believe such things are rebels in the Kingdom of God. We are to love as He has loved us, lose our life for He lost His for us, and give up all for Him who gave up all for us. Giving up all brought Him great joy. "Fixing our eyes on Jesus, the author and perfecter of faith, who for the joy set before Him endured the cross, despising the shame, and has sat down at the right hand of the throne of God" (Hebrews 12:2).

As we give up all, we, too, will find great joy, not pain and loss. Do not allow the enemy to have this foothold; right now with your mouth give up that one thing which is allowing him to steal joy that is rightfully yours. Remember, total surrender is not a point in time when all is given up, but a recognition of a past event: that you are grafted into the Vine, that you are abiding, that you gave up all the day you accepted Him, and, therefore, you are totally surrendered now!

We Have Spiritually Arrived?

As I have emphasized over and over, we are to live our lives moment by moment. Therefore, spirituality is something that is possessed only in the present moment of abiding. The subtle deception of the enemy is that he uses a new truth, freeing though it may be, to make us think that we have at long last arrived at the culmination of Christian maturity. The danger in such thinking is that as we abide we continue to expand, while such a deception does not allow for expansion but will subtly cause us to become dormant. Teachers who take one truth and camp there for very long will with the passing of time find themselves living a carnal existence. The explanation for this happening is really quite simple: Our experiences of the past begin to suffice for life today. The enemy will continue to remind believers of all that happened in the past (even if the past is just yesterday), when it has nothing to do with true spirituality, which must be experienced in this moment.

There is another difficulty with the enemy's persuading us that we have arrived. As soon as we come to the point where we believe we have THE teaching, often we are no longer open to any further teachings or the manifestations of Christ-given gifts in others. An unteachable man is a carnal one.

A pastor from England once reminded me of Matthew 7:13, 14: "Enter by the narrow gate; for the gate is wide, and the way is broad that leads to destruction, and many are those who enter by it. For the gate is small, and the way is narrow that leads to life, and few are those who find it." He explained that on this narrow way that leads to life there are two walls to keep us on the path. One wall is named Arminianism (free will) and the other Calvinism (predestination), and that it does good to bounce off both walls as we go along. How true it is; we need both walls. On the one hand we need to understand the free will of man, and yet on the other, the sovereignty of God. On the one, we need to be firm in our assurance of salvation, and on the other, we need to be warned about being slothful.

As I have mentioned previously, those who enter into true faith no longer find a compelling need to systematize God. Often when speaking about the assurance of salvation that we have in Christ, someone quotes to me Hebrews 6:4-6, John 15:2, and Galatians 5:4, and makes the statement that, "Christians can fall away." That person will then ask me to explain these Scripture verses.

My explanation is simple. "I believe what Hebrews 6:4-6, John 15:2, and Galatians 5:4 teach. I may not understand, but I believe."

Another time someone will begin to quote the Scriptures that teach we cannot fall away (Hebrews 13:5, I John 2:19,

John 10:28) and ask that these be explained in the context of the Scriptures that teach we can fall away. My response is the same, "I believe what Scripture teaches." I do not want to go through all the gymnastics and gyrations that theologians do to change the meaning of a Scripture verse so it will fit into their systems of belief. Nor do I want to attempt to be clever; I am only stating that I do not know all, I do not know the mind of God, and I am not the teacher. Christ alone is the Teacher, and whatever He says I believe, whether I can systematize it or not.

The enemy has persuaded many (of commensurate intelligence, talent, gifts, and spirituality) to choose one wall against the other (causing division), and in so doing, they suffer, for they stagnate. We want to be of those who moment by moment look to the Holy Spirit to reveal what we need for life right then, not what we think we need for our minds. We want life, not knowledge. When this is our attitude, God will reveal what we need to know when we need to know it, and with the knowledge will come life and power.

The Deception of Lying Emotions

As we begin to experience the abiding life, our emotions will take their proper place under the influence of the Spirit. They will begin to express the life of Christ within and will no longer exercise their influence from without, changing our perspective of ourselves and the Lord from one moment to the next. This situation is not pleasing to the enemy, for in dealing with the defeated, he likes to use emotions to get them into the condition of feeling out of fellowship with God, in the hope that with time such false feelings can lead the believers to an ordeal of actually being out of fellowship. The enemy also knows that it is much easier to perpetrate a lie in the emotions than in the mind.

Therefore, it stands to reason that as the emotions are brought under the control of the Spirit, the enemy will work in quiet, hidden, unnoticed ways to bring them back under his influence. To do this, he uses what I like to call "jumping time," which is when our minds return to past events that caused turmoil and our emotions are stirred afresh and applied to the present. One example might be when one is riding along in the automobile and his mind wanders to an event in the past that caused great pain, embarrassment, or loss. As the event is vividly remembered, the emotional turmoil associated with the occurrence also returns, and soon he finds himself having feelings today about an incident that took place years earlier. All of a sudden he is depressed and cannot discern why, for his mind has by then moved on to another thought, but the emotions stirred by the past experience have remained.

Many who have suffered emotional hurts in the past are susceptible to this type of attack from the enemy. It is important to remember that if our emotions are not based upon something specific that we can pinpoint the very moment that we are experiencing them, they are to be rejected.

It Does Not Work?

Often we believe that abiding and walking by faith will bring harmony in every area of our lives. It will, in fact, bring great peace within; however, be assured that the flesh opposes the Spirit. Having this battle resolved within through applying the moment-by-moment cross does not assure that the battle is resolved without. For if we decide to walk after the Spirit, and those with whom we have the most dealings (mates, partners, children, coworkers in the church and at our jobs) are walking after the flesh, there will still be clashes. (I have often observed that marriage partners get along better when both are walking after the flesh than when one decides to walk after the Spirit.) The enemy will use this situation to beat the spiritual believer down and bring him to the place where he feels that it is no longer worth the effort to walk in the Spirit. With this experience comes the thought that it does not work. However, the proof that it does work is the fact that there is a battle between flesh and Spirit. Conflict is being created through contrast.

By walking in the Spirit, you are exercising pressure on those around you, like salt that burns in an open wound. Do not give in to the enemy; the Lord is using you in a mighty way. Allow your life to continue to be leaven to those around you, for what you have has proven itself throughout the centuries to be contagious!

We must also be on guard against judging those who we now can easily see are living a life after the flesh. It is always easy to forget from where we have come and how miserable an existence we were leading. The enemy does not want us to stick it out with others, giving to them what the Lord has given to us. We will, however, by His grace, resist all temptations to turn away from any believer, not being satisfied until we see them raised to victory in Christ. ". . . Freely you received, freely give" (Matthew 10:8).

We Need Not Work?

If we have worked so hard in the past to gain victory, the enemy would now have us doing nothing at all. The life of faith is a life of activity, although there is an immense difference in work that is an expression of our faith and work that is trying to produce faith. The life of Christ within us is always active. "My Father is working until now, and I Myself am working" (John 5:17). As we allow this life to flow, we will be very active. Those who live in passivity, never allowing the life of Christ to be expressed through them, are simply not abiding.

There are many months when a tree appears to be inactive to the naked eye, and yet something is taking place in its innermost parts that will be evidenced in life and fruit. If such life is never overtly manifested, then we could conclude that the tree is quite dead.

The same is true for the abiding Christian; there will be extended periods in which no activity is overtly seen, but in the deepest parts of his being he is being strengthened for the day when life within is made apparent in fruit for those around him. Let me remind you, too, that God does not intend to resolve every manifestation of the flesh through a quick answer. Let me put it another way: Would you rather be a toadstool or an oak? An oak, of course! Even though in the first few hours of the morning the toadstool makes a better showing, it will not last. Many traffic in toadstool solutions, but we will allow the Lord as much time as He sees fit to make us mighty oaks. However, the passive believer who never shows manifestations of life is not abiding, no matter how spiritual he may sound. True faith cannot help but produce work; it is inevitable and cannot be blocked, for faith is from God and possesses His power.

Just as a tree, by the power of its life, can break in two a mighty boulder beside which it is planted, so faith is the power within you that will overcome all obstacles. It is not from you but from Him. Therefore, if you possess faith, it will be manifested. We will not allow the enemy to stifle our faith through the deception of inactivity.

Suggested Reading

Coslet, Dorothy Gawne. *Madame Jeanne Guyon: Child of Another World* (Ft. Washington, Pa: The Christian Literature Crusade). Encouraging life of Madame Guyon, who learned the secret of living an abiding life.

Fenelon. *Let God* (Springdale, Pa: Whitaker House, 1973). Letters written by Fenelon in France during the seventeenth century. Fenelon was the spiritual advisor of a small number of earnest people at the Court of Louis the Fourteenth.

Huegel, F.J. *Bone of His Bone* (Grand Rapids, Mich.: Zondervan Publishing House, 1940). Studies on the indwelling Christ.

Metcalfe, J.C. *In the Mould of the Cross* (Ft. Washington, Pa.: The Christian Literature Crusade). A pen-sketch of the life and ministry of Jessie Penn-Lewis.

Murray, Andrew. *Abide in Christ* (Ft. Washington, Pa.: The Christian Literature Crusade, 1968). Thoughts on the blessed life of fellowship.

_____. *The Believer's Daily Renewal* (Minneapolis, Minn.: Bethany Fellowship, Inc., 1981). Murray explains how to take God with you throughout the day.

_____. *The Believer's Secret of Holiness* (Minneapolis, Minn.: Bethany Fellowship, Inc., 1984). Written to help believers grasp the meaning and importance of holiness.

_____. *The Master's Indwelling* (Minneapolis, Minn.: Bethany Fellowship, Inc., 1977). Studies in self-life and our death with Christ.

_____. *The State of the Church* (Ft. Washington, Pa.: The Christian Literature Crusade, 1983). Murray explains the lack of power within the Church, both its cause and its cure.

_____. *Why Do You Not Believe?* (Grand Rapids, Mich.: Baker Book House, 1979). Thirty-one dynamic messages of faith.

Nee, Watchman, *The Normal Christian Life* (Ft. Washington, Pa.: The Christian Literature Crusade, 1957). Deep insights into our death with Christ on the cross.

_____. *The Salvation of the Soul* (Ft. Washington, Pa.: The Christian Literature Crusade, 1978). Understanding the freedom that Christ wants to bring to man's mind, will, and emotions.

_____. *The Spiritual Man* (Ft. Washington, Pa.: The Christian Literature Crusade, 1968) The definitive work on man's condition at birth being cut off from God, the work of the cross to restore man, and the reality of our new life in Him.

Penn-Lewis, Jessie. *The Centrality of the Cross* (Ft. Washington, Pa.: The Christian Literature Crusade). An excellent book on the work of the cross in the believer's life.

Smith, Hannah Whitall. *The Christian's Secret of a Happy Life* (Old Tappan, N.J.: Fleming H. Revell Company, 1942). Hannah Whitall Smith shares her secrets for living an abundant life.

Taylor, Dr. and Mrs. Howard. *Hudson Taylor's Spiritual Secrets* (Chicago: Moody Press, 1941). The first author to use the term "Exchanged Life."

Trumbell, Charles G. *Victory in Christ* (Ft. Washington, Pa.: The Christian Literature Crusade, 1959). Learning that victory and salvation are both gifts from God.

An Unknown Christian. *How to Live the Victorious Life* (Grand Rapids, Mich.: Zondervan Publishing House, 1966). An excellent book on coming to understand the power of Christ's life within.

Abiding Life Ministries International was founded as a discipleship ministry wherein members of the body of Christ could be trained to minister effectively to defeated believers and unbelievers. This goal is realized through seminars and workshops held in churches throughout the United States and abroad.

If you would like information concerning Abiding Life Ministries' seminars and workshops or the study guide to this book, please check our website, www.abidinglife.com or write:
Abiding Life Ministries International
P.O. Box 620998
Littleton, CO 80162

Other books by Michael Wells include:

Problems, God's Presence, and Prayer, 1993

Abiding Stories, 2005

Heavenly Discipleship, 2006

Untold Stories, Unknown Saints, 2008

My Weakness for His Strength, Volume I, 2011